D0203998

# STRANGERS IN THE HOUSE

# STRANGERS IN THE HOUSE

## The World of Stepsiblings and Half-Siblings

**William R. Beer**

**Transaction Publishers**
New Brunswick (U.S.A.) and Oxford (U.K.)

Library of Congress Catalog Number: 88-22001
ISBN: 0-88738-262-2
Printed in the United States of America

**Library of Congress Cataloging-in-Publication Data**

Beer, William R., 1943–
  Strangers in the house: the world of stepsiblings and half-siblings / William R. Beer.
  p.  cm.
  Bibliography: p.
  Includes index.
  ISBN 0-88738-262-2
  1. Step children–United States. 2. Adolescent psychology–United States. 3. Sibling rivalry. 4. Step families–United States.
I. Title.
HQ777.7.B444 1988                      88-22001
306.8'74–dc19                           CIP

To Duncan, Milly, Jessica, and Denis

*"You won't catch me hanging around when they get here," Adam said. "I'm splitting."*

*"What's got into you? What kind of talk is that?" Charlie sounded sore. "You got a nice little stepsister coming all the way across the ocean and you take off. What kind of thing is that?"*

*"It's easy for you to say," Adam told him. "How'd you like it? A total stranger practically related to you and everything coming into your house and you have to be polite and act like everything's peachy when it isn't? That's not the easiest thing in the world, Charlie. Put yourself in my shoes. It's darn tough. . . ."*

—Constance Greene, *I and Sproggy*

# Contents

# Acknowledgments

This book's preparation lasted from the summer of 1983 through 1986. During that time I was helped by so many people that it would be difficult to thank all of them. I apologize if there is anyone I have forgotten to mention in the following acknowledgments.

Professor Judy DeSena was kind enough to allow me to administer the early version of a questionnaire on stepfamily relations to her sociology classes at Brooklyn College.

Ms. Marsha Dorsky, Ms. Joy Racanelli, Ms. Ronnie Crane and Ms. Sarah Quaglia were of immense help in explaining many of the basic features of stepfamily dynamics, and in allowing me to attend sessions of their stepfamily workshops.

The staff of the Northport Public Library were helpful and diligent in their responses to my frequent requests for interlibrary loans and reference assistance.

My attendance at two of the annual meetings of the Stepfamily Association of America (SAA) was indispensible. The workshops, panel discussions, speakers, and informal conversations provided me with the insights that serve as the basis for this book. I could not possibly list everyone I talked to, so a thank you to the group will have to do. However, I am particularly indebted to Ms. Barbara Mullen, the Executive Director of the SAA. Her tireless and cheerful assistance was priceless.

Ms. Elise Goldstein was of great help in collecting much of the interview material from therapists. My heartfelt thanks to her.

Ms. Maureen Appel, of the Stepfamily Foundation of America and family therapist in Roslyn, Long Island, was generous and unstinting in her assistance from the very start.

Dr. Patricia Papernow, member of the SAA and clinical psychologist in Cambridge, Massachusetts, helped with my understanding of stepfamily issues in ways that I cannot begin to enumerate.

A special note of thanks is due to Brooklyn College Provost Ethyle Wolfe, who arranged for financial assistance at the beginning of this project. I am also grateful to the Research Foundation of the City University of New York for the assistance they provided through the PSC-CUNY Research Award Program.

# Introduction

*"A rich man's wife fell sick and, feeling that her end was near, she called her only daughter to her bedside and said, 'Dear child, be good and say your prayers; God will help you, and I shall look down on you from heaven and always be with you. With that, she closed her eyes and died. Every day, the little girl went out to her mother's grave and wept, and she went on being good and saying her prayers. When winter came, the snow spread a white cloth over the grave, and when spring took it off, the man remarried. His new wife brought two daughters into the house. Their faces were beautiful and lily-white, but their hearts were ugly and black. That was the beginning of a bad time for the poor stepchild."*

—Jacob and Wilhelm Grimm,
*Grimm's Tales for Young and Old*

So begins the Grimm brothers' story of Cinderella, one of our best-known fairy tales of resentment and rivalry between stepsisters. Our folklore is full of stories of stepsisters and stepbrothers, half-brothers and half-sisters, ancient dramas that are re-enacted in the minds of children. But today, the world of stepsiblings and half-siblings is no longer the stuff of fairy tales alone.[1]

It is a real world that urgently needs our understanding, because millions of American children live in it, and thousands more enter it every year. Divorce is so common today that approximately half of those who marry today will divorce, and consequently more and more children see their parents' marriages collapse. A large majority of divorced persons remarry, and their children join them in their new unions. Remarriages create stepfamilies, and stepfamilies are rapidly becoming the new family form in the United States. In 1980 there were

9.6 million American stepchildren, of whom nearly 2 million were living with stepsiblings.

Stepfamilies are not all the same. Sometimes only one partner has been married, sometimes both. Sometimes one partner brings a child or two from a previous marriage and the other is previously unmarried and childless. Some American stepfamilies are extraordinarily complex, with both partners bringing in children from several previous marriages or acquaintances.

Simple or complex, stepfamilies are the wave of the future. They are still poorly understood by professionals, academics, and stepfamily embers themselves. Moreover, what has been written about stepfamilies is mostly from the point of view of the adults in the family, particularly about how to deal with stepchildren and ex-spouses. Seldom are children themselves written about as sentient beings living in a family not of their making, an intimate world not of their choosing.

From the outset, the emotional world of stepsiblings is ambivalent and insecure. Parent and stepparent have found love and companionship, but this happiness is apt to be seen with mixed feelings by the children of the newlyweds. Parental affection, living space, friends, and property are all the objects of intense possessive feelings for children. Often these feelings are the stronger because children have formed close ties to the custodial parent before their remarriage, ties that are particularly binding because they follow the upheaval of bereavement or divorce. A child's acceptance of a stepparent is usually a long and gradual process, if it ever takes place at all.

A stepparent can be held at arm's length by a child, at least at first. But what of a stepbrother or a stepsister? Most modern urban and suburban living quarters being what they are, stepsiblings' entry into a household often means ceding territory that is in short supply, as well as other utilities—bathrooms, televisions, stereos, and telephones, for instance. A stepbrother or stepsister is an invader, who is granted coveted benefits by parental decree. As in the relations between blood siblings, adults can impose solutions and dole out rewards and punishments, but children do not necessarily submit. Solutions that seem reasonable to adults may not meet the needs of the children themselves. Or perhaps more often the new couple cannot come to agreement, or may even be unaware of the children's struggles. By overt and covert tactics, by fair means or foul, the combat continues.

Few relations are as strong and as mixed as those between children in the same family. Brothers and sisters spend most of their early childhoods in conditions of forced and not always harmonious closeness. Rivalries between and among brothers and sisters are so sharp because the rivals are so close, in blood and living conditions, and because they so often think that parental love is finite. Childhood relations with siblings have life-long effects, and people who have not lived through the sibling wars may have missed out.

For rivalry and jealousy are only half the story. Kindness, affection, wise counsel, and examples to be followed are also provided by brothers and sisters. The tender friendship shown a younger child, often following on the heels of a jealous tantrum inspired by real or imagined favoritism for the "baby" of the family, is a bewildering succession of behavior familiar to nearly all parents. Sibling solidarity, in a word, is as important as sibling rivalry. And what a feeling of sharing there can be among children banded together in secret against the world of adult authority! If these tidal emotions of antagonism and solidarity complicate the world of siblings in an intact family, imagine how much more so in the world of stepbrothers and stepsisters.

Over all hangs the possibility that everything will fall apart again; for children of divorce are no longer innocent in this regard. They know that adults can stop loving one another, that a marriage can be shattered and a household torn apart. They have seen it happen before their very eyes. They have a feeling for the transience and delicacy of human emotions that few other people acquire before adulthood. The fickleness of adult affection is often blindingly clear to children during the courtships of single parenthood. They may be repeatedly introduced to a parent's boyfriend or girlfriend, only to have that person disappear after a while. Love and trust, those emotions which children are almost alone able to give spontaneously and unstintingly, are bestowed more grudgingly. So the children may tend more and more to withdraw into a wary indifference, a feigned coolness, in which everyone—adult and peer—is kept at a safe emotional distance. Even more puzzling is the pattern in which children are warm and loving toward a parent's new partner (and his or her children) until the remarriage takes place, whereupon they are suddenly treated as interlopers and competitors.

Children in stepfamilies also feel they have far more power than do children in intact families. Sometimes this power is illusory, since small children often feel that somehow the divorce was their fault and that they are also somehow responsible for keeping the new family together. But in some ways the power is real, because a biological parent may be torn between a new spouse and his or her children. If a stepparent says "It's either him or me!" the parent may very well opt for the child. For the same reason, a biological parent can be used as an ally against stepsiblings. Such age-inappropriate power is frightening to children and can make stepsibling life very rocky as a result. Children's relationships can make or break a stepfamily.

This book has two purposes. The primary goal is to understand relations between children in stepfamilies. At the same time, we wish to analyze what this reveals about the place of the stepfamily in contemporary American society, thereby enriching the sociological understanding of the family. Let us first look at some of the basic dimensions of this world, starting with why the number of stepfamilies is growing so rapidly in the United States today.

## Note

1. See Patsy Skeen et al., "Blended Families: Overcoming the Cinderella Myth," *Young Children* 39 (January 1984):72–74.

# 1

# Stepfamilies in Contemporary American Society

> *"In growing up without the kind of fixed paternal marker that so many boys seem to navigate by, I was able to discover a few things about life, and one of these is that people's comings and goings transcend mere rationalization. Had he tried to excuse any of his actions, my stepfather would only have confused an already bewildering situation. I thank him for not doing so."*
> —Caleb Carr, "An Incident of Wolves"

For better or worse, the stepfamily is the family of the future. If present trends continue, before the end of this century the stepfamily will be the largest single type of family in the United States. How did this come to pass?

Almost all stepfamilies today are created from divorce and remarriage; those that follow from the death of a spouse account for a relatively small proportion of stepfamilies. In 1960, 22 percent of remarriages involved widows, compared to only 9 percent in 1980.[1] Not only are there more divorces but because of improvements in health and longevity, today most parents are not widowed until after their children leave home. And in the bereaved population women far outnumber men, reducing the likelihood that they will remarry. Thus nowadays, in contrast to the past, divorce is usually in the background of step-sibling relationships.

To begin our exploration of the world of stepbrothers and stepsisters, we must look first at some reasons for family instability in the United States. We are at a turning point in family organization, where our families are changing to accompany changes in the broader society and economy. The "nuclear family," consisting of two parents and their dependent children, is typical of urban, industrial society. But as societies enter a "post-industrial" phase, families change as well. Single-parenthood, in which mothers are unmarried, is increasingly common, and some divorced parents will remain single. But most single mothers and divorced parents eventually do marry or remarry, and both create stepfamilies, which may well be the typical family form of post-industrial society. The link between these changes in family structural and overall societal change needs to be explained.

In the United States until quite recently, the most common family type was the nuclear family. In many ways, this kind of family is much weaker than in the past. Today the family is no longer the focus of most economic activity, and outside agencies carry out jobs that families once performed. For instance, schools and day care centers now educate and nurture children, tasks once done exclusively by family members. At the other end of the life span, pension plans and life insurance take care of the elderly, once exclusively the job of children and grandchildren. In many ways, the nuclear family is more efficient in industrial society: it is small, it is mobile, and can follow the shifting needs of the economy and changing job opportunities. But it has drawbacks.

Perhaps the nuclear family's greatest drawback is its instability. If a parent in an extended family is lost by death or desertion or (very rarely) by divorce, the children of the couple still have a stable family structure. In addition to the remaining parent, uncles and aunts, and grandparents and siblings, help fill in the void. Painful though such a loss might be, the family is not overturned by it. But in the nuclear family, there are no other adults immediately available to take the place of the missing parent, no resident grandparents to absorb the impact, and a veritable upheaval has taken place. This upheaval becomes more likely in light of the reasons why most Americans get married in the first place.

One of the most peculiar things about families today is that they are formed from a marriage between two people who choose their partner because they are in love. The idea of romantic love as a basis for marriage is a uniquely modern phenomenon. Romantic love in other historical eras was seen as more of an affliction than a blessing. In ancient Rome, it was farcical when a blindfolded Cupid stung a person randomly with his arrows, causing him to fall in love with someone absurdly inappropriate. In that greatest love story of all time, Romeo and Juliet, the lovers are star-crossed because their families hate each other, their love is forbidden, and the story cannot possibly have a happy outcome. For most of Western history, romantic love has been seen more as something ridiculous or tragic rather than something to be sought out.

Thus at first sight, it is bizarre that romance should not only have come to be seen as a desirable state, but should also actually be used as a basis for making a life-long commitment. But perhaps it is not so strange at that. As the family's economic importance declined, it was almost inevitable that economic motives for marriage would also decline. The rise of the nuclear family was accompanied by the appearance of personal compatibility as a basis for marriage. In the nuclear family, we invest much more of our total selves in the choice of a mate. As a result, the possibilities of mutual emotional satisfaction are vastly greater, perhaps for the first time in human history. The possibilities of failure are equally great. As romance replaces economics as a basis for marriage, disappointment can more easily lead to divorce. Remarriage is more likely to the extent that adults expect spouses to fill all their emotional and sexual needs. From this perspective, then, stepfamilies are one result of our culture's strong emphasis on adult romantic fulfillment.

Divorce has always been a possibility, but in the last twenty years, it has become increasingly probable. The recent explosion of the divorce rate requires an explanation in its own right.

### Divorce in the United States Today

About half of all marriages in the United States today end in divorce, and the likelihood of divorce has increased enormously in the last thirty years.[2] Why is there so much divorce in our country today? One explanation is that we simply live much longer than we did a century ago. In the past, to stay married "until death us do part" was not a difficult promise to fulfil, since few men and women lived beyond the age of thirty-five or forty. As life expectancy has gone up, the time we live with a spouse has lengthened, and the sheer possibility of disaffection has grown.

The lives we enjoy now also have new phases that did not exist in earlier times. We have more than the brief periods of childhood, youth, marriage, childbearing, and death, of which people's lives in the past were composed. The extended period of courtship involved in adolescence, for instance, exposes each of us to a large number of members of the opposite sex; memories of them do not necessarily fade once we have decided whom we will marry. Middle age is a time of far greater duration, during which people are in close proximity in work and leisure with members of the opposite sex who may present themselves as potential alternate partners. Old age is not the brief and disease-ridden prelude to death that it once was. Courtship, sexual activity, and new marriage now can and do continue in this phase of life. Thus in our longer lives we are presented with far more chances to compare members of the opposite sex with our present spouse, and the comparisons are not always flattering.

Laws pertaining to divorce have been considerably eased in most states in recent years.[3] Easier divorces lead to more divorces, and more divorces lead to more acceptance of divorces. Acceptance, in turn, leads to even more divorces. During the 1970s, when the divorce rate was exploding, between 40 and 50 percent of Americans thought that it should be more difficult to get a divorce. But during the same time about 30 percent of Americans thought that it should be *easier* to get a divorce. Evidently, some Americans are disturbed about the colossal rate at which marriages are collapsing, but many think laws should be changed to make marital breakups easier.[4]

Our expectations of marriage are far higher than at any other time in history. If we expect a marriage partner to be a lover, sexual partner, friend, workmate, co-parent, and helper in all the practical tasks of everyday life, it is likely that a spouse will fall short in one or more of these areas. So we are more likely to seek a better relationship if these raised expectations are not met. This means that marriage as an institution is not necessarily in crisis, as some have put it, but in fact is improving. The high divorce rate is not a sign of the deterioration of marriage but of the greater expectations we have of it. Such modern marriages, so the argument goes, are much more satisfying than the cool and distant partnerships that last a lifetime.[5]

The increase in divorce is also partly due to women's greater participation in the labor force. Since World War II there has been a tremendous influx of women into higher and professional education. This has meant that they are better prepared for work outside the home and thus more economically independent. Until the post-World War II era, most married women were essentially dependent on their mates for support. Single women spent little time in school, devoting their energy primarily to cultivating domestic skills and finding a husband, or at most working only until they got married. Hence women were generally ill-suited to independence in the world of work. This had an obviously discouraging effect on divorce, because despite personal unhappiness and marital incompatibility, many women hesitated to try to strike out on their own.

All this has changed. At present, there are somewhat more women than men of college age enrolled at universities. Single women can support themselves as long as they want to and are not under the economic pressures of the past to find a man to support them. The age at which women first marry has increased markedly since 1950. This gives marrying women higher levels of work experience in addition to their generally higher levels of education. And after marriage they are much more likely to continue working. More than half of all married women now work outside the home. One result of these changes is that if a marriage is unsatisfactory, there are far fewer economic obstacles to divorce in a woman's way, although divorce does still produce substantial hardship, particularly for mothers.[6]

There is a clear relation between overall changes in economic prosperity and the incidence of divorce. A recent and exhaustive study found that when economic conditions improve, marriages *and* divorces increase; when conditions deteriorate or when the rate of improvement slows, people hold back on these decisions.[7] People divorce less when the economy is less healthy; in 1982-84, divorces declined slightly because of relatively difficult economic circumstances. In 1985, with the return of prosperity, the rate of divorce started to go up again. The U.S. has undergone dramatic economic growth since World War II, which may also help to explain why divorce has become so common.

The feminist movement has also encouraged divorce by attacking the family itself. Many outspoken feminists are hostile to the institution of marriage altogether. Susan Brownmiller holds that the origin of marriage is rape, because in marriage, women choose one rapist to protect them from other rapists.[8] In a popular paperback, Eva Figes wrote that marriage is a "hollow sham."[9] Catherine Mackinnon maintains that marriage is the "organized expropriation of women's sexuality and work.[10] In *Radical Feminism* we read that in marriage, wives are owned by their husbands in the sense that "slaves are owned by their masters."[11] And let us not forget Gloria Steinem's famous dictum that a woman needs a man like a fish needs a bicycle.

The number of children involved in divorces has exploded. In 1955, it was reported that 347,000 children witnessed their parents' divorce. Two decades later, the figure was 1.1 million in a single year—the number of children caught up in divorces had more than tripled. In 1981, the number climbed still further, to 1.2 million. Two fifths of all children born to married women will witness the breakup of their parents' marriage before they become adults. The older a child is the more likely he is to experience the divorce of his parents, but even for infants, the home is increasingly likely to be broken up. One quarter of all children under the age of two now experience divorce.[12]

### Remarriage and the Formation of Stepfamilies

Divorce does not discourage most people from marriage, at least not for long. More men than women get married again: 83 percent of divorced men remarry, and 76 percent of divorced women.[13] Women's remarriage rates are lower because of age; older women are less likely to find partners.[14] Having children by a previous husband does not, in itself, substantially reduce a woman's remarriage prospects. The end result is that more and more children become stepchildren every year. According to a study published in 1982, it is estimated that 1,300 stepfamilies with stepchildren are being formed *every day*.[15] Another recent report, based on the 1980 Current Population Survey, says that there were 2.2 million stepfathers in 1980 and 338,000 stepmothers. Stepfathers outnumber stepmothers because women get custody of their children in the overwhelming majority of divorce settlements. In the same year, there were 150,000 people who were both stepmothers and stepfathers, that is, remarried couples who had both brought children from a previous marriage into the present marriage. Most important, in 1980, one out of five children under eighteen living in married couple households were living in stepfamilies.[16]

Once a stepfamily is formed from a remarriage, though, there is no guarantee that it will not be torn apart again by divorce. It is estimated that half of all remarriages end in redivorce.[17] On the average, redivorce occurs after about six years.[18] One recent analysis concluded that almost half the children who go through a divorce and remarriage will also undergo the breakup of the new family. Within two years after their parents' remarriage, 15 percent of American children witness the breakup of the new household. Within five years, 28 percent of children in remarried families see redivorce occur. And by the time ten years have elapsed since the formation of the stepfamily, a staggering 46 percent undergo a second parental divorce.[19] These figures probably underestimate the problem of redivorce, because they do not include people who are no longer children by the time their remarried parent redivorces. Simply on the basis of probabilities, the stepfamily does not seem to any more stable than the biological family.

The emerging marriage pattern is one in which a woman will have a child, either in or out of wedlock, by a man she is likely to live with for a period of time. They will separate or divorce, and the chances are overwhelming that she will be granted custody of the children. There follows a period of single parenthood, followed by courtship, and ultimately cohabitation with a new partner, with or without the benefit of marriage. This new partner may bring children of his own from one or more previous liaisons. It is possible that the woman will also have a child with her new partner. This new marriage is no more likely to last than the previous one. She may redivorce, will probably retain custody of the offspring, and may well marry a third time. Thus, the marriages of the future will increasingly be "serial" marriages, in that they will take place in a series, one after the other.[20] These marriages are monogamous, because men and women form relationships with one person at a time and, occasional adultery aside, remain with that partner exclusively until divorce. This is why the new pattern of marriage in America is referred to as "serial monogamy."

Serial monogamy is the marriage trend of the future—whether comprising one, or more than one, divorce and remarriage. The family produced by these marriages is known by a more familiar name: the stepfamily. This book's background hypothesis is that the stepfamily is a family form well matched to post-industrial society. This kind of society is typefied by an emphasis on personal freedom and emotional fulfillment, sexual experimentation and egalitarianism, a reduced importance of kinship and consequent salience of nonfamily agencies that care for and educate the young, nurture the elderly, and carry on almost all economic activity. This theme is taken up again in the conclusion and examined in light of the book's findings.

Black U.S. stepfamilies are not analyzed below because among blacks the incidence of single-parent families, divorce and desertion, remarriage and redivorce all follow patterns so different from those of whites that they form a distinct kinship system that deserves treatment by itself. The high rate of single motherhood increases the prevalence of black stepfamilies because most single mothers marry, but usually not to the fathers of their children.[21] Black children also experience divorce far more often than white children, and experience redivorce more often.[22] The stepfamily is not only much more common among blacks, it has existed as a common alternative to the nuclear family for a century or so.[23] The black stepfamily is thus probably more institutionalized; white stepfamilies have much to learn from their black counterparts.

Among the majority population, stepfamilies formed from single parenthood and divorce are fairly new, and as a result few realize the extent to which they differ from nuclear families.

### What is a Stepfamily?

⊁ A stepfamily can be most simply defined as a family in which at least one member of the adult couple is a stepparent.[24] Although it can be defined fairly easily, the contemporary American stepfamily is such a new phenomenon that we cannot even agree on what to call it. It has been variously called the remarried family, the reconstituted family, the blended family, the synergistic family, the combination family, the barbell household, and the binuclear family.[25] While some of these terms may be preferable, the terms "stepfamily" and "step" are used in this book simply because they are the most commonly accepted terms.

The term "stepfamily" actually includes a wide variety of different types of remarried families, some of which are simple and others complex. The simplest type of stepfamily is one in which a divorced or bereaved spouse with one child remarries a new, never-married, childless spouse. The most complex stepfamily is one in which both remarrying spouses bring children in from previous marriages, as well as having a child or children together—so-called mutual children. The most complex of these stepfamilies still only results from one set of divorces and one set of remarriages. If any of the remarriages is followed by redivorce and re-remarriage, which is a distinct and growing possibility, the complexity of the stepfamily increases geometrically. Ex-spouses remarry, too, to persons who have spouses by previous marriages, and who also have mutual children of their own. This produces an extraordinarily complicated network of family relationships in which adults have the roles of parent, stepparent, spouse, and ex-spouse; some adults have the role of custodial parent and others have the role of noncustodial, absent parent. The children all have roles as sons or daughters, siblings, residential stepsiblings, nonresidential stepsiblings, residential half-siblings, and nonresidential half-siblings. There are two subtypes of half-sibling roles: those of children related by blood to only one of the adults, and the half-sibling role of the mutual child. Children also have stepgrandparents and ex-stepgrandparents as well as grandparents.

Complex or simple, the stepfamily differs from other families in clearly discernable ways.[26] Here are the most important:

1. Nuclear families are simple in structure, and they essentially have only one typical pattern: mother, father, and dependent children. By contrast, *the structure of any stepfamily is complex*. Consider, for example, that there are eight different types of remarriages (divorced man, single woman; divorced man, widowed woman; divorced man, divorced woman; single man, divorced woman; single man, widowed woman; widowed man, single woman; widowed man, widowed woman; widowed man, divorced woman). For each of these there are three theoretically possible types of parent–child patterns (father and children and new stepmother, mother and children and new stepfather, father and his children and mother and her children). There are thus at least twenty-four different possible patterns in a stepfamily (even though some may be unlikely, such as a single father with children). The remarried couple may or may not have one or several mutual

children, adding complexity. Moreover, some stepsiblings may live together permanently, some may visit regularly, and others may be absent. Other complications are added by varying numbers and sexes of siblings, stepsiblings and half-siblings, ages of children (and hence their birth-order and birth-interval). Making the different types of stepfamily even more complicated is the presence of in-laws and stepgrandparents, not to mention the potential added complications of divorce and remarriage.[27]

2. The nuclear family is usually thought of as a relatively static institution, with a set number of players acting within fairly clear roles. As long as divorce, death, or the birth of a new child does not change the composition of the nuclear family, we think of it as composed of the same mother, father, and children. To a much greater degree, *the stepfamily is a process*, with a changing cast of characters living in a household at any one time.

I began my in-depth interviewing of one stepfamily with a question about who the family members were. The response was a confused look and the question, "Well, when do you mean?" I learned that the family has consisted of at least three different households with different spouses and children who live with the family for a while and then live either with another adult or move out on their own. Even grown children sometimes return to live at the main household for varying lengths of time. Stepfamilies are like a trolley car that rolls along the tracks, with people getting on and off. The family continues, but the characters who make it up constantly change.[28]

3. The membership of a nuclear family is relatively clear. Although there are degrees of relationship, ranging from the immediate blood and conjugal relatives through in-laws to distant cousins, it is usually easy enough to say who is a member of the family and who is not.[29] But in the stepfamily, boundaries are not clear. The answer to "Who is in the family?" may depend on whom you ask. If a child's custodial mother remarries, her new husband becomes that child's stepfather. The child may or may not perceive such a stepparent as a member of the stepfamily. What if the child's noncustodial father remarries? His "stepmother" may think of herself as part of his stepfamily but the child may not. If this stepmother should have had children from a previous marriage, are these children stepsiblings, even though he may rarely see or visit them? What of the noncustodial stepmother's parents? Are they "stepgrandparents?" The child may feel they are and the grandparents may not, or vice-versa. These questions, confusing as they are, only take a stepfamily at a given period of time. Stepfamily membership becomes even more cloudy when a parent and stepparent

redivorce. If a stepparent divorces one's parent, does that person cease to be a member of the family? None of these questions can be precisely answered.[30] This has led some analysts to talk of the "meta-family system," which includes "the stepfamily, former spouses, grandparents, stepgrandparents, aunts, and others who may have significant input into the stepfamily system."[31]

4. In the nuclear family, the rules are known. Common sense, religion, and laws provide an elaborate and explicit (though at times difficult and contradictory) set of norms about how people are supposed to act. There are no such generally accepted expectations of people in stepfamilies: roles and relationships are undefined. This is mainly because the stepfamily is not yet recognized as a social institution in its own right. It is a *non-institution*, which means that its patterns of behavior are not clearly understood or accepted by the participants or the society at large.[32]

The problem of discipline illustrates this ambiguity. A child in a stepfamily has difficulty sorting out to whom he is to be obedient. He must obey the custodial parent, but obedience to the stepparent is not automatic. The frequent cry is "You can't tell me what to do! You're not my mother/father!" The children have a point. They must obey their non-custodial parent when visiting, but what if that parent's rules are very different? If the non-custodial parent remarries, must a child obey the new spouse? If so, just how far does that obedience go? At the least it is a temporary form of obedience, which puts all obedience to parents into a kind of conditional mood that most children in other types of families do not encounter.

5. The familiarity of the rules in a nuclear family has its counterpart in the law. The legal obligations of nuclear family members toward one another are fairly well recognized by lay persons. But in spite of jurists' effort to bring it up to date, the law is confused with regard to the stepfamily. The law is a reflection of, but not identical with, social norms. As society changes, so do laws, more slowly and with their own logic. Laws about stepfamilies are confused, but this is only a reflection of the general social confusion.

For instance, in the conventional family a man is normally responsible for supporting his children, and under some circumstances his wife may be as well. But a stepfather has no legal obligation to his stepchildren; instead, their support is normally provided by their father. Since noncustodial fathers are not always reliable in their payment of child support, a stepfather finds himself financially at the whim of an absent male outside the home. Visitation rights held by the non-custodial parent further cloud a stepparent's responsibility, and noncustodial parents can have severely disrupting effects on a stepfamily by arbitrarily changing their plans for visitation at the last minute. The role of the stepparent is precarious; the relationship between a stepparent and stepchild only exists in law as long as the biological parent and stepparent are married. If the biological parent dies, the stepparent instantly loses any legal claim to custody over his stepchild(ren), and custody reverts back to the surviving biological parent. The only way for a person to cement his or her legal tie to stepchildren is by adopting them, but this requires the cooperation of the noncustodial parent, which may not always be forthcoming. To state it simply, there is no *single legal "center of gravity" in the stepfamily.*[33] This has important financial consequences for stepfamilies, among others.[34]

6. Rules and laws are clear for nuclear families and confused for stepfamilies; this lack of clarity is reflected in our lack of adequate terms to describe steprelations. Our language has relatively few kinship words, and in a stepfamily, the same word has to denote very different relationships. The word "stepmother" applies to a woman married to a father with whom a child lives, but is also supposed to apply to a woman who has married a child's mother's ex-husband, whom the child may see rarely, if ever. It also is used to refer to the new spouse of an elderly parent who may have been bereaved; in such a case a person may never expect to have any but the most passing acquaintance with the stepmother. "Stepmother" is thus an inadequate word used to denote three entirely different types of relationship.

The children of one's resident parent's new spouse are stepsiblings. But so are the children of a non-residential parent's new spouse. If one's resident parent and stepparent have a child together, that person is a half-sibling. But the same term is used for the mutual child of an absent and rarely-seen parent and his or her new spouse. Here again, the same word is used to describe different relationships. Furthermore, there are no words at all for some stepfamily relationships. For example, John and Mary divorce. Mary is remarried to George. John is remarried to Carolyn. George and Carolyn have a kinship link to one another. They may see each other frequently, such as in negotiating the visitation of the stepchildren. But there is no word in English for the relationship between these two family members.

If we cannot talk clearly about a relationship, we cannot think clearly about it, and the lack of clear stepfamily terms in our language seriously hampers the acceptance and understanding of stepfamilies themselves.[35]

7. A nuclear family is formed gradually, over time. It usually begins with courtship, which is followed by marriage and child-bearing, with

the birth of children spaced over a relatively extended period of time. Members of a nuclear family, in short, have time to get used to it and one another. But a stepfamily is a ready-made family, in which there is no prior opportunity for members to adjust. Instead, in a stepfamily, adjustment must come after the family is formed.[36]

A stepchild expressed some of the emotional implications of this post-marriage adjustment in the following terms:

> Now my father is remarried. At first I was shocked because my father was living with this other lady. Then he decided he was going to move. I thought he was just going to live by himself. So I went over there and there was this lady who came in. I was like, 'Who is this?' So he introduces me. He doesn't tell me anything. Then, my stepbrother who was there, he tells me my father was going to marry her. I was like, 'Wait a minute, Why didn't my father tell me this?' I was so angry at him. I was so mad because she just suddenly jumped into our lives. You know, I was ready to just be with my father for a while. . .''[37]

Stepchildren can actually exert a centrifugal force, deliberately or unconsciously attempting to subvert the new marriage in hopes of reuniting their parents.[38]

8. The emotional world of the nuclear family is complicated, but at the outset it is based on hope and optimism. For the most part, people decide to begin a new family because they believe that their relationship is strong enough to last over time and through the stresses and strains of everyday life. At the beginning of the stepfamily, certainly, there is hope, but many stepfamily members are also likely to feel *guilty*. Parents' feelings of failure may be compounded because the pain of divorce is most difficult for children to bear, and parents must feel that they have directly contributed to their children's suffering. The previously single stepparent may also be subject to feelings of guilt (depending on the circumstances of the divorce) at having provoked the breakup of the family.

> "For the [previously single] marital partner, this former spouse may be the object of intense emotions that include jealousy, rivalry, feelings of triumph, and guilt regarding feelings of triumph. One new stepmother said guiltily, 'I was the other woman, fifteen years younger, and everyone knows it.' ''[39]

Children are no strangers to guilt in post-divorce stepfamilies. Children frequently feel that somehow the divorce was their fault. And as soon as the stepfamily is formed, they are torn by feelings of disloyalty for the absent parent if they start to feel love for the stepparent. Joining a stepfamily, for a child, means showing disloyalty to the absent parent.

Such loyalty conflicts are reported to be the most serious source of difficulty by adolescent stepchildren.[40]

When the stepfamily results from bereavement, guilt can result from a surviving spouse's feeling of having betrayed his deceased partner by remarrying. Children also feel guilt at feelings of affection for a stepparent because they feel disloyal to their dead mother or father.

9. A nuclear family begins afresh, and its participants are going through their adjustments for the first time. But in a stepfamily most or all of the participants have undergone a "loss" of someone near to them, through either death or divorce.[41] And both children and adults are grieving the death of the family. Social scientists studying death and dying have found that grieving goes through stages, and there is evidence that the grieving of a divorce goes through stages analogous to those following death. Ideally, by the time a bereaved or divorced parent remarries he or she will have completed the process of grieving, but this is not necessarily so. It is very likely that the children will not have finished grieving the loss of the family and will be expected to accomplish the difficult task of adjusting to life in the stepfamily before they have gotten over losing their previous family. In fact, remarriage can activate grief for children because it means relinquishing the dream of reuniting parents.

10. In a nuclear family, there are myths that need to be reconciled with the reality of family life: no spouse is perfect, children do not necessarily turn out to be angels, home life is not as it is depicted in Norman Rockwell paintings. But the realities are not so far different from the ideals that we cannot strive to reconcile them. In the step-family, the same myths are dangerous because it is impossible to make a stepfamily into a family like any other. This produces two dangerous myths that impede the formation of a cohesive stepfamily, the " myth of instant love," and the "myth of the recreated nuclear family."[42]

Both of these myths are particularly difficult to overcome in light of the guilt discussed in the previous section. A divorced parent will try— this time—to succeed as a parent and a spouse. The more a remarried person tries to make the stepfamily into a family like any other, the more he is going to fail. A stepfamily cannot begin to be successfully formed until the couple ceases to pretend that they are in a nuclear family.

In sum, there are at least ten fundamental ways in which the step-family is different from the nuclear family: complexity, a changing cast of characters, unclear boundaries, undefined roles, unclear laws, a lack of kinship terms, the "instant family," pervasive guilt, persistent griev-ing, and the myth of the recreated nuclear family.

## Stepsiblings: The Neglected Dimension

Most attention to stepfamilies focuses on solving the problems of being a stepparent. Insofar as children themselves are dealt with, they are considered incidental to the parental tasks of keeping the family together. This is understandable. A remarrying parent seldom has a realistic perception of just what he or she is getting into. Overwhelmed by the unanticipated burdens of stepparenting, adults seek counsel. Counselors, for good reason, focus on the cohesion of the remarried couple because, as one put it, "If you don't have the couple, you don't have the family." The energies of adults are thus usually concentrated on their own immediate tasks, and their relationships with each other and with the children take priority. Usually lost in the shuffle is the nature of relationships between children themselves.

A look at the books in print on the subject confirms this judgment. Andre Bustanoby's *The Readymade Family: How to be a Stepparent and Survive* (Zonderman, 1982), Elizabeth Einstein's *The Stepfamily: Living, Loving & Learning* (Shambala, 1985), Leslie Kaplan's *Coping with Stepfamilies* (Rosen Group, 1985), Ruth Roosevelt's *Living in Step* (McGraw, 1977), and John and Emily Visher's *Stepfamilies: Myths and Realities* (Citadel, 1980) are popular accounts for stepparents, inter-larded with advice. There are more formal guides for adults in step-families: Erna Paris' *Stepfamilies: Making Them Work* (Avon, 1985), and John and Emily Visher's *How to Win as a Stepfamily* (Contemporary Books, 1983). There are also guidance manuals for children themselves. These include Getzoff and McClenahan's *Stepkids: A Survival Guide for Teenagers in Stepfamilies* (Walker, 1984) and Janet Stenson's *Now I Have a Steppparent and It's Kind of Confusing* (Avon, 1979), but these deal with stepsibling and half-sibling relations only in passing and do not analyze their dynamics. The Vishers also have a guide for family therapists who are treating stepfamilies, *Stepfamilies: A Guide to Working with Stepparents and Stepchildren* (Brunner and Mazel, 1980), and another therapist, Jamie Keshet, wrote *Love and Power in the Stepfamily: A Practical Guide* (McGraw-Hill, 1986). There are two sociological studies of the stepfamily as a system, but one (Lucille Duberman's *The Reconstituted Family: A Study of Remarried Couples and Their Children*, Nelson Hall, 1985) was first published over ten years ago, and the other (Burgoyne and Clark's *Making a Go of It: A Study of Stepfamilies in Sheffield*) focuses on stepfamilies in a British city. Similarly, Elsa Ferri's *Stepchildren: A National Study* (Taylor and Francis, 1984) does not study stepchildren in the U.S.[43]

Stepsiblings are therefore evidently the neglected dimension in stepfamilies. The neglect of stepsiblings parallels the lack of attention to sibling relations in intact families. Surprisingly, in the immense body of literature on family relations, only a tiny amount focuses on relations between siblings.[44] Yet anyone who has lived in a family in which there are siblings knows that a great deal of what goes on in the family takes place between youngsters, and parents may only be dimly aware of some dramas being played out in the home. The tone and atmosphere of a family, and even its success or failure, can be deeply affected by sibling relations. One anthropologist was so convinced of the importance of sibling relations that he held that the brother-sister relationship is the core of the family as we know it.[45] The network of relationships that is built up between brothers and sisters influence a person's personality, his roles as an adult, and his relations with his peers.[46] Living with stepsiblings is equally important.[47]

Even though the stepfamily is very different from the nuclear family, we must use sibling relations as a starting point for exploration of stepsibling relations. Four general areas appear to be most important.

*Rivalry*

Rivalry between siblings is a central feature of family life. The competition derives from a fear that parental love is finite, and that love bestowed upon a brother or a sister will reduce the love one receives. Its manifestations are many, perhaps the most familiar being children's insistance on "equality," that all children receive equal amounts of food or attention or presents, since these are symbols of love.[48] Children persist in their rivalry in spite of repeated parental assurances that they are all equally loved.[49]

Less attention has been given to the equally important reality of sibling solidarity. Some research has shown, though, that sibling support is an important aspect of family networks, especially when people are in middle and older age. The death of parents, in particular, can be a catalyst bringing brothers and sisters together in later life. Whatever the occasion, sibling networks can be nourishing and supportive. They certainly deserve to be better understood.[50]

Thus, the first area of relations between siblings in stepfamilies that this book will explore is the area of stepsibling rivalry and its corollary, stepsibling solidarity.

*Age Order*

There has been much speculation on the effects of order of birth, and consequently age-order, on a child's role within the family, and on it subsequent effects in later life. Whether a child is first born or a middle child or the "baby" of the family is very important to children themselves, and often to adults as well. Some evidence shows that birth- and age-order, particularly the status of being the oldest child, also have significant effects on one's personality.

Combination stepfamilies consist of two sets of siblings merged by remarriage. In this event, there is always some change of position in the age hierarchy for one or more of the stepsiblings. The second topic is thus the effects of a change in age-order upon stepsiblings.[51]

## Sexuality

Rules governing sexual behavior are fundamental to the cohesion of the family. Most important is the prohibition of sexual relations between any members of a family except the parents: sex between generations is forbidden, as is sex within the generation of young people in a family. Observing the "incest taboo," as this rule is called, is indispensible to the successful functioning of any family.

Stepfamily relations call into question many assumptions about sexual taboos, most particularly those concerning sex between unrelated stepsiblings. Sexual issues were cited among the greatest sources of stress by adolescents in stepfamilies.[52] The third major issue to be discussed, therefore, is the issue of erotic attraction between stepsiblings.[53]

## Birth of a Half-Sibling

In the lives of children in a nuclear family, the birth of a new child has important emotional consequences, particularly losing status as the youngest in the age-order. Regressive behavior stemming from jealousy, exhibited especially by the child who was youngest (or the only child) up to that time, is the most familiar result.

In a stepfamily, the birth of a child to parent and stepparent has far more serious consequences. On the one hand, it can mean intensified feelings of competition and loyalty conflict, but on the other it can serve as a symbol that the stepfamily really has a future, and is more than just a temporary living arrangement. The newly arrived half-sibling, too, has a crucial role in the stepfamily. Accordingly, the fourth aspect of stepsibling relations to be analyzed is the effects of the birth of a half-sibling.[54]

## Description of the Studies Done for This Book

Since stepsiblings have hardly been studied at all, the research for this book was exploratory because at the beginning it was not clear what kinds of questions had to be asked. It was based on six different types of inquiry: a review of the literature, a pilot study and interviews with family therapists, interviews with adult stepsiblings and half-siblings, in-depth interviews with five stepfamilies, participation in three stepfamily self-help groups, and a survey of stepfamilies in whose households were living stepsiblings and/or half-siblings. What follows is a brief explanation of how the information for this book was gathered.

### Review of the Literature

The published material on stepfamilies was studied, in a search for material directly dealing with stepsiblings and as a source of hypotheses. As indicated above, little has been published directly dealing with stepsiblings. In the indirect references to the subject, four themes recurred: stepsibling rivalry, changes in age-order, stepsibling sexuality, and the role of half-siblings.

Thus, although the review of the literature revealed little information about stepsiblings, it did provide initial guidelines for research.

### Pilot Study and Interviews with Therapists

Published material is second-hand, and in the initial stages of research, others who have dealt with stepfamilies first-hand were consulted. This consultation took two forms, a mailed pilot study of family therapists who dealt with stepfamilies containing stepsiblings, and direct interviews with such counselors. In the pilot study twenty-seven responses were obtained. In the direct interviews twelve family therapists were interviewed in depth about the four areas and the author's major hypotheses.

### Interviews with Adult Stepsiblings and Half-Siblings

In-depth interviews were conducted with twenty young adults who had grown up as stepsiblings and/or half-siblings. These interviews took at least an hour, dealing with the issues at length. Only persons who had grown up with stepsiblings or half-siblings living in the same household were interviewed. Respondents were identified by means of advertisements placed in the Brooklyn College student newspaper and on the Brooklyn College radio. This group comprised non-clinical respondents, in that they were persons who had grown up as stepsiblings and/or half-siblings, but did not suffer from emotional disturbances serious enough for them to seek treatment for it. They were thus different from the clients normally seen by the interviewed therapists.

*Interviews with Stepfamilies*

Since the young adults interviewed about stepsiblinghood could only talk from their personal point of view, an in-depth study of five non-clinical stepfamilies was carried out. In each of these cases, each of the residential members of the stepfamily was interviewed for a perspective on its interpersonal relations. These interviews were, for the most part, tape recorded and transcribed.

*Participation in Stepfamily Self-Help Groups*

Recently stepfamily self-help groups have proliferated throughout the United States. They consist of stepfamily members who are not so disturbed as to seek counseling or therapy, but who are aware of the serious challenges posed by stepfamily living, realize they need help, and want to share support and information. As in the previous two cases, the subjects were non-clinical; although the stepfamily members who go to the groups realize that they need help and support, a self-help group is quite distinct from group therapy. The groups are normally under the supervision of a social worker who has been trained in stepfamily issues, but serious pathology is not dealt with during the meetings. The author attended five sessions of one group, six sessions of another group, and almost all the sessions of a third group for six months. For reasons of confidentiality, the names and locations of the groups must be withheld.

*Survey of Stepfamilies*

The Stepfamily Association of America is a self-help group for stepfamily members, with sixty chapters throughout the country. Questionnaires eliciting open-ended responses were sent to chapter chairpersons. They were asked to give the questionnaires to chapter members in whose households stepsiblings and/or half-siblings were living. A total of thirty questionnaires were returned, most with extensive descriptions of stepsiblings dynamics.

None of these six approaches by itself would have been sufficient, but taken together they served as a basis for providing the initial approaches to the stepsibling and half-sibling experiences presented in this book.

## Notes

1. United States Bureau of the Census, *Statistical Abstract of the United States* (Washington, D.C.: U.S. Government Printing Office, 1980), p. 80.
2. See Paul Glick and Arthur Norton, "Frequency, Duration, and Probability of Marriage and Divorce," *Journal of Marriage and the Family* 33 (May 1971):307–17. See also Theodore Caplow et al., *Middletown Families.* (New York: Bantam, 1983), p. 16. and "U.S. Divorces Drop," *Facts on File* (New York: Facts on File, 1985), p. 209, G2.
3. Richard Neely, *The Divorce Decision: The Legal and Human Consequences of Ending a Marriage* (New York: McGraw-Hill, 1984), p. 6.
4. United States Bureau of the Census, *Social Indicators III* (Washington, D.C.: U.S. Government Printing Office), p. 40, tab. 1/2.
5. Cited in Robert Wernick, *The Family* (New York: Time-Life, 1974), p. 135.
6. See Lenore Weitzman, *The Divorce Revolution* (New York: Free Press, 1985), esp. p. 338.
7. Alex Inkeles, "The Responsiveness of Family Patterns to Economic Change in the United States," *Tocqueville Review* 6 (Spring/Summer 1984):5–50, esp. 32.
8. Susan Brownmiller, *Against Our Will* (New York: Simon and Schuster, 1975), p. 7.
9. Eva Figes, *Patriarchal Attitudes* (New York: Stein and Day, 1972), p. 179.
10. Catherine MacKinnon, *Feminism Unmodified: Discourses on Life and Law* (Cambridge, Mass.: Harvard University Press, 1987), p. 49.
11. Anne Koedt et al., *Radical Feminism* (New York: Quadrangle, 1973) p. 219.
12. Larry Bumpass, "Children and Marital Disruption: A Replication and Update," *Demography* 21 (February 1984):71–82.
13. Paul Glick, "Remarriage: Some Recent Changes and Variations," *Journal of Family Forces* 1 (March 1980):455–78. See also Hugh Carter and Paul Glick, *Marriage and Divorce: A Social and Economic Study*, (Cambridge, Mass.: Harvard University Press, 1970), p. 239.
14. Andrew Hacker, *U/S: A Statistical Portrait of the United States* (New York: Viking, 1983), p. 112.
15. Census Bureau figures reported in the *New York Times*, Monday, 24 October 1983. But see Andrew Cherlin and James McCarthy, "Remarried Couple Households: Data from the June 1980 Current Population Survey," *Journal of Marriage and the Family* 47 (February 1985):23–30.
16. Ibid. According to Cherlin and McCarthy, there were 7.6 million remarried couple households in June of 1980. This figure only includes those households with less than six children. It does not include 512,000 households in which women had six or more children.
17. United States Bureau of the Census, "Current Population Reports: Number, Timing, and Duration of Marriages in the United States," no. 297

(Washington, D.C., U.S. Government Printing Office, 1976). See also Selina Prosen and Jay Farmer, "Understanding Stepfamilies: Issues and Implications for Counselors," *Personnel and Guidance Journal* (March 1982): 393–96, and Alan Booth and Lynn White, "The Quality and Stability of Remarriages: The Role of Stepchildren," *American Sociological Review* 50 (October 1985):689–98.

18. Glick and Norton, 1971, *Frequency*.
19. Bumpass, 1984, "Marital Disruption."
20. See Andrew Brooks, "Repeated Remarriage: A Growing Trend?" *New York Times*, 7 February 1985.
21. David Mills, "Stepfamilies in Context," in *Relative Strangers: Studies of Stepfamily Processes*, ed. William Beer (Totowa, N.J.: Littlefield-Adams, 1988).
22. Bumpass, 1984, "Marital Disruption," 74, 80.
23. Jo Ann Manfra and Robert Dykstra, "Serial Marriage and the Origins of the Black Stepfamily: The Rowanty Evidence," *Journal of American History* 72 (June 1985):18–44.
24. Kosinski, "Improving Relationships in Stepfamilies," *Elementary School Guidance and Counseling* 17 (February 1983): 200–7.
25. "Reconstituted" is used by Lucille Duberman, *The Reconstituted Family: A Study of Remarried Couples*, (Chicago: University of Chicago Press, 1975); "blended" may be found in Fitzhugh Dodson, *How to Parent* (Los Angeles: Nash, 1970); "synergistic" is coined by Davidyne Mayleas, *Rewedded Bliss: Love, Alimony, Incest, Ex-Spouses, and Other Domestic Blessings*, (New York: Basic Books, 1977). "Combination" refers to a particular type of stepfamily, in which both parents bring children from previous marriages, as described in Gerda Schulman, "Myths that Intrude on the Adaptation of the Stepfamily," *Social Casework* 53 (March 1972): 131–39; "barbell household" was used by Paul Bohannon in his *Divorce and After*, (New York: Doubleday, 1968). "Binuclear" was invented by Constance Ahrons, "The Binuclear Family: Two Households, One Family," *Alternative Lifestyles* 2 (Fall 1979):499–515, and was also used by Paul Bohannon, "The Binuclear Family," *Science 81*, (November, 1981):2 and passim.
26. See also Harriet Johnson, "Working with Stepfamilies: Principles of Practice," *Social Work* 25 (July 1980):304–8; Terry Perkins and James Kahan, "An Empirical Comparison of Natural Father and Stepfather Family Systems," *Family Process* 18 (June 1979):175–83.
27. For an excellent discussion of stepfamily complexity, see Esther Wald, *The Remarried Family: Challenge and Promise* (New York: Family Service Association, 1981), pp. 87–112.
28. See Sharon Price-Bonham and Jack Balswick, "The Non-Institutions: Divorce, Desertion, and Remarriage," *Journal of Marriage and the Family* 42 (November 1980):959–972, esp.
29. Kenneth Walker and Lillian Messinger, "Remarriage After Divorce: Dissolution and Reconstruction of Family Boundaries," *Family Process* 18 (June 1979):185–92. See also Len Fink, "Losing Stepchildren When a Marriage Comes Apart," *Newsday*, (January 22, 1985):7.
30. Prosen and Farmer, 1982, *Understanding Stepfamilies*, 393–97, esp. 394.
31. Ibid. p. 393. See also Caplow, et al., 1982, *Middletown Families*, p. 339.

32. Andrew Cherlin, "Remarriage as an Incomplete Institution," *American Journal of Sociology* 84 (November 1978):634–50. See also Price-Bonham and Balswick, 1980, *The Non-Institutions*, p. 967; Andrew Cherlin and Frank Furstenberg, "The American Family in the Year 2000," *The Futurist* 17 (June 1983):37–41; and Peter Watrous, "Step-Etiquette," *Psychology Today* (January 1984):80.

33. "Parent and Child" in *American Jurisprudence* (2nd ed.) 59 (Rochester, New York: Lawyers Cooperative Publishing Company, 1987), p. 136, par. 2.

34. Stan Albrecht et al., *Divorce and Remarriage* (Westport, Conn.: Greenwood, 1983), pp. 142–43.

35. See William Beer, "Toward a Typology of Stepkin," paper presented at the Annual Meeting of the Eastern Sociological Society, 1985.

36. Claire Berman, *Making It as a Stepparent: New Roles, New Rules* (Garden City: Doubleday, 1980), p. 50. This is why, among professionals counseling and treating stepfamilies, the emphasis is upon identifying the stages that stepfamilies must go through after they are formed in order successfully to adapt. See for example, Jane Ransom et al., "A Stepfamily in Formation" *American Journal of Orthopsychiatry* 49 (January 1979):36–41; David Mills, "A Model for Stepfamily Development," *Family Relations* 49 (July 1984):365–72; and Patricia Papernow, "The Stepfamily Cycle: An Experiential Model of Stepfamily Development," in Ibid., pp. 355–63.

37. Children's Express, "Kids Compare Notes," *Ms.* (February 1985):49.

38. Margaret Nelson and Gordon Nelson, "Problems of Equity in the Reconstituted Family: A Social Exchange Analysis," *Family Relations* 31 (April 1982):223–31.

39. Emily Visher and John Visher, "Common Problems of Stepparents and Their Spouses," *American Journal of Orthopsychiatry* 48 (April 1978): 252–62.

40. Patricial Lutz, "The Stepfamily: An Adolescent Perspective," Family Relations 32 (July 1983) 367–75.

41. From Doris Jacobson, "Stepfamilies: Myths and Realities," *Social Work* 24 (May 1979):202–7.

42. Ibid., p. 203; see also Schulman, 1972, *Myths* pp. 133–39.

43. One published work on stepsiblings is Elinor B. Rosenberg and Fady Hajal, "Stepsibling Relationships in Remarried Families," *Social Casework* (May, 1985):287–92.

44. Brian Sutton-Smith and B.G. Rosenberg eds., *The Sibling* (New York: Holt, Rinehart and Winston, 1970); also Michael Lamb and Brian Sutton-Smith eds., *Sibling Relationships: Their Nature and Significance Across the Lifespan* (New York: Erlbaum, 1982). See also Jay Schvaneveldt and Marilyn Ihinger, "Sibling Relations in the Family," in Ivan Nye et al., *Contemporary Theories About the Family* (New York: Free Press, 1979).

45. Ralph Linton, *The Study of Man* (New York: Appleton-Century-Crofts, 1936), p. 159.

46. Stephen Bank and Michael Kahn, "Sisterhood-Brotherhood is Powerful: Sibling Subsystems and Family Therapy," *Family Process* 14 (September 1975):311–37. See also Jane Pfouts, "The Sibling Relationship: A Forgotten Dimension," *Social Work* 21 (May 1976):200–4.

47. Mary Whiteside and Lynn Auerbach "Can the Daughter of My Father's

New Wife Be My Sister?'' *Journal of Divorce* 1 (Fall 1977):271–83, esp. 278ff.

48. Sigmund Freud, "The Development of the Libido and the Sexual Organization," *Complete Psychological Works of Sigmund Freud*, 16 (London: Hogarth, 1963), pp. 333–34.

49. Linda Craven, Stepfamilies: *New Patterns in Harmony* (New York: Julian Messner, 1982), p. 108.

50. Kenneth Walker and Lillian Messinger, "Remarriage and Divorce: A Review," *Social Casework* 58 (May 1979):276–85, esp. 284.

51. Elizabeth Einstein, The Stepfamily: Living, Loving, Learning (New York: Macmillian, 1973), p. 72, Lucille Duberman, "Stepkin Relationships," Journal of Marriage and the Family 35 (May 1973):283–92, esp. 291.

52. Patricia Lutz, "Stepfamilies: A Descriptive Study from the Adolescent Perspective," *Dissertation Abstracts International*, 1980, p. 992.

53. Emily Visher and John Visher, *Stepfamilies: A Guide* (New York: Brunner and Mazel, 1979), pp. 176–77.

54. Einstein, 1973, *Living, Loving, Learning*, p. 75ff. and Visher and Visher, 1979, *Stepfamilies*, p. 78.

# 2

# Sharing Parental and Stepparental Affection (and Almost Everything Else)

> In the course of time Cain brought to the
> Lord an offering of the fruit of the ground,
> and Abel brought of the firstlings of his flock
> and of their fat portions. And the Lord had
> regard for Abel and his offering, but for Cain
> and his offering he had no regard. So Cain
> was very angry and his countenance fell. The
> Lord said to Cain, "Why are you angry, and
> why has your countenance fallen? If you do
> well, will you not be accepted? And if you do
> not do well, sin is crouching at the door; its
> desire is for you, but you must master it."
> —Genesis, 4:3–7

Stepsiblings, like all siblings, must share space, property, possessions, and, above all, parents. Sharing the love, attention, and approval of parents is never easy and often creates deep and lasting competition among brothers and sisters. As in so many other regards, the stepfamily is much more complicated in this area because absent parents and stepparents add sources of competition between children. For instance, stepsiblings, unlike siblings, have a presumptive adult ally in their biological parent, whereas a blood sibling cannot automatically claim one parent's solidarity in competition with another sibling.[1] These rivalries are also more complex because they take place between children who do not see each other as having the same legitimacy in their claim to scarce resources such as love, space, and property.

One commentator says that, whereas in nuclear families, triangular rivalries are based on a bedrock of love and loyalty, the rivalries in a stepfamily may be more destructive until the people involved acquire a common family history. She avers that stepsibling relations are fundamental, saying, ". . . the better the relationship between stepbrothers and stepsisters, the stronger the family."[2] We should also remember, though, that stepsibling rivalry is not necessarily contradictory to the eventual outcome of valued relationships because, in the words of two other researchers, "The rivalries [between children] seemed somewhat keener. . . but the friendship patterns were more valued."[3]

To introduce the patterns of stepsibling rivalries, let us first look at the stories of Pete Gilbert and Brenda Goldberg.

### Pete Gilbert

Pete Gilbert is a twenty-two-year-old college student. When he was nine years old, his mother died, and for five years he lived with his father and his older sisters, Kristin, Theresa, and Freya, who were respectively eight, five, and three years older than he. An aunt lived upstairs, and she helped his sisters take care of him. When Pete was eleven years old, his father started dating Leah; three years later, after talking it over with his four children, his father remarried. Leah had five children by a previous marriage: Susan (nine years older than Pete) was soon engaged and left the home. Larry, eight years older, joined the Marines. Sophie, ten years older, was already living with someone elsewhere. Sean, seven years older than Pete, had already drifted away from his family. Finally, there was Max, who was the same age as Pete.

The whole stepfamily, then, consists of Pete's father, his stepmother Leah, his three sisters (Kristin, Theresa, Freya), his two stepsisters (Susan and Sophie) and his three stepbrothers (Larry, Sean and Max). But many of the youngsters had left or were about to leave the home by the time the remarriage took place. With Theresa away at college by then, the household consisted of the two adults, Pete's sister Freya, Peter, and his stepbrother Max. It remains that way to this day, and although Max is away at college, he returns every weekend and lives there during the holidays.

Pete remembers that living in the stepfamily was at first hard for both him and Max. "The new family was tough for him. It was hard on me, too. I was the youngest and could have pretty much everything I wanted. Then to share it and have to live in the same room with him was really tough." So Pete and Max had to share two precious things right from the start—being the youngest and their bedroom.

The battle lines were soon drawn. "It started out, 'This is your area and this area is mine. Whatever's mine you don't touch.' " At least there was no sharing of clothes, because Pete is bigger than his stepbrother. Even though they were hostile from the beginning, there was no real physical fighting, as Pete remembers. "To this day I can't have a discussion with him, because he doesn't want to discuss anything we do."

For the most part, during those adolescent years, "We ignored each other. I lived my life and he lived his." This mutual avoidance continued even though they went to the same high school. "We went through four years of high school without going to the same classes, because he's an idiot."

Different intellectual levels were not the only thing that kept Pete and Max separate in spite of their being roommates. "We were both on the track team, but we had different events. I was in long distance and field events, and then went into field. Max was in intermediate distance."

"I had more girls, but he had a longer relationship with someone. Now it's reversed—I've been going with the same girl for five years, and he doesn't have just one girl but is going out with someone different every week." They also like different kinds of girls. "Max likes big girls, very tall with big butts. I don't." As far as music is concerned, Pete and Max used musical tastes to differentiate themselves, too. Both of them love music, but very different kinds. "Back when disco was the thing, you were 'into disco,' it was 'what you were.' So Max was disco and now he's new wave. I was heavy metal and now I'm rock and classical." A few tastes really are dissimilar; Pete likes poetry and literature, but Max does not like to read much.

When he graduated from high school, Pete decided to go away to Arizona to college. His decision had a lot to do with his relationship with Max. At that time, Max did not know what he wanted to do, and went to the local community college. Pete's father had retired and was around the house a lot.

> It got to be a big hassle. I wanted to get out of the house. . . . I had been living with Max for four years and watching his attitude towards me. It was getting to the point where I was going to do something I didn't want to do, like kick the shit out of him. His attitude was arrogant, irresponsible, antagonistic. In that situation [living in the same room] I couldn't ignore him.

> Also, I wanted to go out and see things. I had lived in my home town all my life. I'd never really been away, and couldn't just run back whenever I felt like it.

But Pete did come back at the end of the year to live at home and go to college nearby. "There's no way to get away other than walking out, but when you come back, it's still there."

Pete's older sister Freya, the third person in the young triangle, was a firm ally of Pete's. Relations between Max and Freya were, if anything, worse than between him and Pete. "Freya was antagonistic towards anyone but me. I could say or do anything I wanted and she would accept it. Today, the only person Freya is close to is me. Freya and Max were antagonistic from the beginning." Thus, in the continuing struggle between the two young men, Pete had the decisive advantage of a coalition between himself and an older sister.

Although the central dialogue is clearly between the two stepbrothers, the stepfamily is still hanging together as a loose coalition of blood and non-blood siblings, their spouses and children. "I see my stepsisters and other stepbrothers more often now. Sophie got married and has a baby. I see her about once a month. She's the only [stepsister] I like. Sophie is most like my mother" in that she is concerned about his well-being. Larry is still in the service, has married and is a father; Pete sees him and his infant son fairly often. "But he's not like Kristin's child. I carry Kristin's child's picture in my wallet, but not Sophie's." How about Sean? "Sean was always a problem, because I liked him, only because he seemed the most honest of all my stepbrothers. But his biggest problem is he's a drug addict, and I was told not to talk to him or be alone with him. For the first couple of years he wasn't there."

All in all, Pete's recollection of those turbulent adolescent years was one of simultaneous solitude and close confinement with Max. "Back then, I couldn't even talk to my father. I had to work most of these problems out myself. There was the adolescent fear of feeling stupid, not wanting to bring him petty stuff." He had no guidelines from peers for how to conduct his relations with his stepbrother, either. In fact his friends seem not to understand his experience. His best friend, for instance, has an older brother with whom he doesn't get along. He said to Pete, "You're lucky Max isn't your brother, so you can hate him!"

### Brenda Goldberg

Brenda Goldberg is a twenty-three-year-old college student from Maryland. She has a younger brother, Victor, and an older sister, Joan. Her father divorced her mother when she was six years old; at that time, Victor was five and Joan was eight. Her mother had been declared incompetent by a court, and except for a brief period during which she and her siblings lived with her, Brenda and her siblings subsequently lived with their father. He remarried soon after and moved to Minnesota and, later, Iowa. Brenda's stepmother's ex-husband lived in California. In the new stepfamily, Brenda had a stepbrother (Frederick, aged twelve) and a stepsister (Felicity, aged nine.) Her stepmother had an adopted daughter (Daisy, aged eighteen) who also joined the stepfamily. Three years after remarrying, her father and stepmother had a mutual child, Millie. Before the remarriage, her stepmother had retained custody of her stepsiblings for about two years, but during that time Frederick and Felicity had spent most of their time in boarding schools. Brenda grew up in the stepfamily from age nine on; she moved out of the house when she was eighteen, but lived nearby for the next five years. Six months ago, she moved to Baltimore by herself to go to college and, since it was less expensive, she lived with her grandmother.

*Author:* What were the relationships like at the beginning of the stepfamily?

*Brenda:* Frederick was very resentful. We weren't allowed to call my stepmother 'Mom.' He would say, 'That's *my* Mom, not yours.' From day one he couldn't stand us. He was vicious until we stood up to him. Our parents were always going out—they were married after two weeks—and left Frederick in charge. My little brother was a funny looking kid, so he got most of it, especially because he shared a room with Frederick. Victor was five when we moved in with them. He had to make Frederick's bed. There was a slave–master relationship between them. Victor said he hated it, but he grew up to be a lot like Frederick.

*Author:* Let's look at the relations between the pairs of children in the family as you were growing up. How about your relationship with Felicity?

*Brenda:* In the first year, Felicity resented us, too. After about a year, we became close. I idolized her. She's a nonconformist. We have a lot in common. It's somewhere between friendship and sisterhood, it's a mixture of both. We're definitely sisters, but different. . . . Felicity is a play-type sister. Joan is a sister-sister. Felicity got me my first date. If I had a problem, I'd go to Joan. She's like a mother to me. She was protective, but we fought the most. She was like a mother. Now we're real close. And we have nothing in common.

*Author:* How did the two of them, Felicity and Joan, get along?

*Brenda:* Felicity and Joan were always competing with friends. They always had the same friends. They didn't compete for grades.

*Author:* Did you ever get along with Frederick?

*Brenda:* No, we were never close. He was always hostile.

*Author:* You've mentioned the relationship between Frederick and Victor. Could you tell me a little more about it?

*Brenda:* After a while, Victor started helping Frederick. Frederick started using Victor as a tool against all of us.

*Author:* How about the other relationships?

*Brenda:* Frederick and Joan? They were indifferent after a while. She was the first to stand up to him. As for Victor and Felicity, it was total indifference, but Joan and Victor were very close.

*Author:* How did the children react when Millie was born?

*Brenda:* I thought it was neat. We were tighter than tight. Incredibly close. I'm closer to her than any of the others.

*Author:* How about the other children?

*Brenda:* Frederick and Felicity didn't like Millie at all [at first]. Eventually Frederick liked her but didn't admit it. Millie was spoiled rotten when she was little. Felicity had the relationship with Mom [Brenda's stepmother] until Millie came along. Felicity [eventually] loved mothering Millie.

*Author:* What kind of relationship was there between your stepsiblings and their father?

*Brenda:* He was rich and lived in California. They used to visit him once a year, in the summer. They would go to California and play in the sun and have fun. He would send a huge box of presents to them from everyone on that side. I always felt jealous that he sent presents to Frederick and Felicity and not to us. Christmas was the occasion when there was a big box, a giant box from California with about 20 million presents in it.

*Author:* Did the stepsiblings ever crow about getting the presents?

*Brenda:* No.

*Author:* Was there a brother or sister or stepbrother or stepsister that you wanted to be like?

*Brenda:* I idolized Felicity. . . . She always did crazy things. She never worried. Mom liked her best. I wanted Mom to like me, so I decided to be like Felicity. It didn't work. It's painful. Mom used to say to Felicity, 'Don't grow up to be like Brenda' [even though she was slightly older]. I was singled out by her. We stepkids got hit, but the biological children were not. . . . I was always aware that my stepmother was not my mother. The jealousy with the box of presents underlined that. But I always thought of my stepsiblings as siblings.

The stories of Pete Gilbert and Brenda Goldberg illustrate one of the most important aspects of the relations between stepsiblings—that of rivalry. In order to examine more deeply the specific character of stepsibling rivalry, we must first look at jealousy and competition in families that do not include the complications of steprelationships. With that as background, we can look at the ways in which stepsibling rivalry is similar and different.

## Sibling Rivalry

It is no accident that the story of Cain and Abel is near the beginning of the Bible: competition between brothers and sisters is as ancient as the human family. God's finding more favor with Abel's sacrifices was sufficiently painful to Cain that he was visibly crestfallen. In response, God gave him hard but sound psychological advice. He had to learn to master the feelings that came as a result of losing out in competition with his brother. If he did not, he would be faced with the temptation to do evil. Cain did not succeed in controlling his hatred for his competitor, and as we all know, in the end he murdered him. We can regret that Cain did not succeed in absorbing God's advice, but few of us who grew up with brothers or sisters can fail to recognize the feelings described. On many occasions, our "countenances have fallen," because we lost out in some sibling struggle.

Commentators have seen Cain and Abel as symbols, standing for husbandry versus nomadism, or the desert versus the field. But the story is symbolic in yet another way. It seems clear that we can also look at their competition for favor in the eyes of the Lord as a displaced version of their competition for favor in their father's eyes. Losing out in this contest, therefore, means much more than simply having one's offering spurned; it means a lack of regard for the work one has put into making oneself lovable. Cain's defeat was not just a loss of love, it was a loss of regard for the best he had to offer.

Rivalry between siblings begins as soon as a new child arrives on the scene. (Remember that Cain was Adam and Eve's first born.) Prior to that event the older child was the sole possessor of parental love, of living space in the house and all the other rights and privileges of being a child. The older child feels displaced as the center of attention and removed from a preeminent position. The younger child feels relatively powerless and defenseless in the face of sibling wrath and reacts defensively and competitively.

Parental love is the central bone of contention. Although the pretexts may vary, beneath all the issues is the fear that parental love might run out, that the more love is shown a sibling the less there will be for oneself. The world of sibling rivalry is a gigantic zero-sum game in which one side's gain is the other side's loss. It makes little difference if parents insist that they love their children equally. Such assurances may temporarily reduce the heat of animus but cannot extinguish the fire. The only solution to the problem of sibling rivalry is the psychological development of the children to the point where autonomy and social competence override the anxieties of parental abandonment. And even when they are adults, competition between siblings can remain extremely keen.

What seems most intractable about sibling rivalry is its pervasiveness. Children's insistence about absolute equality in distribution of foods, gifts, parental time, money, space, and dozens of other prized items all revolve around their being symbols of parental love. Most other subjects of competition between siblings are byproducts of this rivalry. Sibling rivalry is therefore both simple and complex. It is simple in the sense that it has an origin which is easily traceable to competition for parental love. It is complex in the sense that it shows up in many ways that symbolize parental love to the participants, though this is not immediately obvious to onlookers. In short, parental love is the prize, but almost anything can be seen as a sign of that prize.

Competition between siblings also shows up in another more obvious form. Siblings will vie with one another in their efforts to establish themselves as independent persons, competing according to standards set by themselves or peers. In the psychoanalytic sense, the two types of competition are indistinguishable. But while the first is unwinnable because it is so irrational and so intractable, the second provides more positive outcomes. It is hard to win in the struggle for parental love in any but the most ambivalent sense; any victory is likely to be seen as temporary, and in any case is fraught with guilt and fear of retribution. In struggles whose standards and rules have been set by siblings or peers, it is at least possible to win. Or even when winning is not a clear result, the effort to differentiate oneself from siblings is a way of harnessing hostility and using it to establish one's autonomy, acquire a sense of one's abilities, and to approach some solution to the quest for identity. In the words of one researcher:

> "Thus even when children feel equally loved and accepted by parents. . . . the intersibling struggle for recognized competence and status includes an ever-widening range of abilities and attributes. The struggle for parental rewards per se becomes less crucial. Siblings are viewed as prime targets for social comparison, not only within the family system but throughout the child's expanding extrafamilial social system."[4]

Sibling rivalry is most acute in childhood, when the familial arena is the most important sphere to a child, and the issue of parental love is the only important thing or is certainly the most salient. Nonetheless, rivalry between siblings does not vanish as soon as a person has grown to maturity and left the home. The memory of early struggles remains, and both mythology and literature are full of the themes of competition between siblings in later life.

Psychological studies also reflect the continuing nature of sibling rivalry in later life. For instance, in one study focusing on sibling rivalry among adults, it was found that almost three quarters of a group studied experienced one of two types of rivalry. The first was *adult-initiated,* by which the authors meant that it showed up either in overt or covert comparisons made by parents between children. The second was *sibling-generated,* confirming the appearance of new rivalries beyond simple competition for parental affection. Some adults felt that parents still showed favoritism toward one child or the other. Some siblings persisted in acting competitively toward one another. Some felt as if they were excluded from family interactions. And some still felt stigmatized by continued assignment of negative labels that had been affixed to them in childhood. The weapons used in these rivalries included achievement outside the family, physical attractiveness, intelligence, interpersonal competence, and maturity. Sometimes the rivalries were relatively simple, consisting only of the envy of one sibling with regard to another. In other cases, they consisted of a reciprocal contest, where siblings tacitly agreed to continue comparing themselves with each other. In still other cases, the rivalries were sex-linked, in that there were greater degrees of competitiveness between siblings of the same sex than siblings of the opposite sex.[5]

### Stepsibling Rivalry

Stepsibling rivalry is just as strong as sibling rivalry, but it has different textures. For a look at its basic themes, let us first consider the following dialogue between the author and a group of youngsters ages six to fourteen. All have stepsiblings and/or half-siblings.

*Author:* How do you feel when people live together who are not brothers and sisters?

*Dina:* It's uncomfortable. My sister thinks because I'm not her real sister that I hate her. Then we fight and she goes off and cries, 'You hate me! You hate me!'

*Author:* Do you get the feeling that it's us and them? [This had been the theme of a group discussion earlier.]

*Paul:* Sometimes. Dad is the switchboard operator.

*Mary:* My stepbrothers don't like me and they play with my brothers. And I cry because I have nothing to do. We're not supposed to watch television on weekends, but my Mom lets me because I have nothing to do.

*Virginia:* Tanya and Carol [her stepsisters] have Jap clothes and I don't, and they go to a Jap school and I don't cause I'm not Jewish. My stepfamily's Jewish and my family's Christian. They talk about Jewish things and I ask what they're talking about and they say if you were Jewish, you'd know so we won't explain.

*Sophie:* Me and my stepbrother don't consider ourselves brother and sister. We're friends.

*Author:* What kinds of things do you get jealous about?

*Dina:* When we've spent time with our [noncustodial] Mom, we come home with lots of presents, and Kim [her stepsister] gets jealous, and we get into fights.

*Author:* Do your parents ever try to go in the other direction, and try to be harder on their own children than steps?

*Paul:* Not really. Once.

*Dina:* Except Kim's [Dina's stepsister] rules were different, because she was with our stepmom, and they're more familiar to her. So it's a little harder on her.

*Craig:* My dad tries to treat us all the same, but when he treats us just a little differently, it's overriden by my stepmother. We have to do things her way. She always gets her way. You can tell Dad doesn't like it.

*Author:* What won't you share with a stepbrother or stepsister?

*Dina:* Things from my mother's side of the family. Like one morning I went into Kim's room and saw my great-grandmother's sheets on *her* bed!

*Author:* What else won't you share?

*Chorus of Voices:* A room!

*Virginia:* You don't want to share a room, because if you have friends over, your little sister comes in and bugs you. Friends are private.

*Dina:* I don't share friends with my stepsister.

*Author:* Did you want this, or did it just turn out that way?

*Dina:* [firmly] We just don't share friends.

*Paul:* I have nothing whatever to do with my stepbrother. I talk to him about once a month. When he's in the house, I'm not, and when I'm in the house, he's not.

The ages and the sexes of the children in this conversation varied, as did their custodial arrangements, the ages at which they entered their stepfamily, and the amount of time they had lived in a stepfamily. But some basic themes of stepsibling rivalry emerged in spite of these differences.

From the outset, there is a perception that it is "us" and "them;" there is no instant love between stepsiblings. The description of a parent as a "switchboard operator" is particularly apt. The parent is the conduit, since the parent is married to the other children's parent. When differentiation between stepsiblings by blood is reinforced by cultural and religious differences, as in the case of Christian and Jewish stepsiblings, the gap can become even wider.

With such distances as background, we can take a look at the actual issues. The first is that of different rules. Parental rules are an essential part of a family's culture, and passing from one set of rules to another can produce a culture shock as great as that of going to live in a foreign country. One of the ways in which stepparents attempt to deal with these differences is to impose all the rules impartially, yet we know that they cannot always succeed. When Craig's father tries to show any partiality, Craig sees his stepmother as imposing uniform rules, and that his dad is not always pleased with this equity. Dina's observations are equally perceptive. Her stepsister Kim lived with Dina's stepmother, and thus is more familiar with the rules. But Dina astutely says that this may be harder on Kim. These rules are imposed both on Kim herself and on Kim's stepsiblings. Neither Craig nor Dina, it would seem, are pleased by the evenhandedness shown regarding rules; impartiality regarding family rules may not be accepted by stepsiblings. Although scrupulous "equality" would seem to be one way in which sibling rivalry can be even temporarily allayed, equity among stepsiblings is not always seen as fair if only because the rules are almost always more familiar to one set of children than the other.

A second issue that emerges is that of money and presents from an absent parent. When Dina goes to visit her mother, who does not have custody, she returns laden with gifts. Kim remains home with her own mother, and does not benefit from such parental largesse. This case of inequitable distribution of prized resources cannot be controlled by Kim's mother. Yet Kim feels understandably deprived because she does not have a generous absent parent, and the ensuing stepsibling rivalry is of a sort that usually does not arise among biological siblings.

Third, there is the crucial issue of space. As we saw in the discussion of Pete Gilbert and his stepbrother Max, the "indigenous" children feel invaded and the "invaders" feel like interlopers. Nobody is comfortable.

Closely related to living space is the problem of possessions. Objects acquire meaning when we see them as ours; they have even more significance when they are bones of stepsibling contention. Dina's example is telling in this regard. From her point of view, Kim did not deserve to have Dina's great-grandmother's sheets on her bed. A bed is an intimate place, and the juxtaposition of a stranger with a symbol of a relative was clearly distasteful to her.

Finally, there is the theme of sharing friends. Because our relationships with friends are the subject of intense proprietary feelings, it is not suprising that stepsiblings are as reluctant to share friends as possession and rooms. Dina states categorically that she does not share friends with her stepsister. Virginia says simply, "Friends are private."

Just from this brief interview with a group of stepchildren, certain aspects of stepsibling rivalry emerge. There is the feeling of membership in distinct groups based on blood, with the parent serving as the switchboard operator between the groups. Attempts at uniform enforcement of rules are not necessarily seen as fair by stepsiblings. When as absent parent is generous during visitation, the good fortune of the returning children is envied by stepsiblings. The main issues of com-

petition for this group of youngsters seem to be living space, possessions, and friends.

At times the objects of competition are blood relations themselves.
Stepfamily literature is full of references to children's jealousy of stepsiblings' use of familiar terms, like "Mom" or "Dad" for a parent.
"That's *my* parent, not yours!" is the oft-repeated cry. A child, too,
can resent a stepsibling's closeness to the child's own sibling. One
young woman interviewed described her younger teenaged sister's
problems with drugs, alcohol, the police, and promiscuity. She attrib-
uted part of this to her sister's resentment of the closeness between
herself and her stepsister. "She loves her, but she was sad and jealous
when I went from sharing a room with her to sharing a room with [my
stepsister]. I don't remember why, but [my stepsister] and I got very
close, and I think that's part of my sister's problem also. I guess that
she maybe felt like [my stepsister] was taking me away from her."

### What Stepparents Say About Stepsibling Rivalry

Accounts of individual stepsiblings are one way to look at the recurring themes of stepsibling rivalry, but like most case studies, they
provide a lot of information about a very restricted number of people.
In an attempt to get a more comprehensive picture, a set of questions
relating to stepsibling rivalry was asked in a mailed survey of members
of the Stepfamily Association of America (SAA). One of the questions
identified the subjects of major conflict between children in the family.
Respondents were asked to circle the items that seemed to be grounds
for conflict, and then to describe in detail what these conflicts were
like.

Some respondents said that there were no major conflicts between
children in the household. When they did indicate that there were
conflicts between stepsiblings and/or half-siblings, though, certain items
were repeatedly circled more than others. The results of the survey
are presented in Table 2.1. In order, the most frequently mentioned
subjects for conflict were over sharing parents' affection, property, a
room, stepparents' affection, friends, and parents' time. Conflict over
sharing money from an absent parent and sharing money from a stepparent was hardly mentioned at all. Two other items were mentioned
three times each by parents: conflicts over chores and responsibilities
in the household, and conflicts over affection and time spent with
grandparents.

How do the parents themselves describe these stepsibling rivalries?

TABLE 2.1
Major Sources of Conflict among Stepsiblings as Reported in Survey of
Stepfamily Association of America

|  | Number of Times Cited | Percent of Total |
|---|---|---|
| Sharing a room | 7 | 14 |
| Sharing property | 9 | 17 |
| Sharing friends | 5 | 10 |
| Sharing parents' affection | 10 | 19 |
| Sharing parents' time | 5 | 10 |
| Sharing stepparents' affection | 7 | 14 |
| Sharing stepparents' time | 4 | 8 |
| Sharing money from parent in household | 3 | 6 |
| Sharing money from absent parent | 0 | 0 |
| Sharing money from stepparent | 1 | 2 |
| Total | 51 | 100 |

*Rivalry over Parental and Stepparental Affection*

"Major conflicts occur over the natural [i.e. biological] and stepparents' time to do things with them."

"My wife's son is particularly close to his mother and gets possessive of her time. He requires a lot of her attention."

"The sharing of space, property, and *attention*. The space and property [conflicts] seem to be simply that they have never had to share in the home—only with friends. The attention [conflict] seems to be related to the stepparent and having to share time with their biological parent."

"My husband frequently does [errands] on Sundays and takes his son to help him. My daughter wants to go instead of my stepson some of the time and resents that she isn't offered first choice. My husband's parents shower my stepson with money, affection, gifts, and time. My daughter is generally ignored by them and since she has no grandparents she frequently resents the situation."

"There are five children in our household—the conflicts tend to involve the perception that one child is favored more than others."

"There were no blatant conflicts. There were more feelings from my husband's children that my children had gotten most of the time [that should have been] for them. There were undercurrent feelings of jealousy. My children are achievers and my husband's son felt he could not measure up."

### Rivalry over Property

"Personal property is important, and they are more possessive. It seems to me that the normal conflict between regular siblings is more exaggerated in a stepsibling situation. It tends to be more manipulative to the parents than in normal traditional siblings."

"There is an ongoing problem with jealousy over who got what clothes and personal items."

### Rivalry over Sharing a Room

"Our two youngest boys share a room. Conflict arises when the youngest uses his older stepbrother's belongings without asking or invades his privacy."

"My two sons, ages eight and thirteen, share a room while their stepsister has her own room. The boys used to have their own rooms, and resent the fact that now they do not."

"Two teenage boys in one small bedroom just causes tension and irritability. Also, problems [arise] over who gets to use the room for homework and who has to use some other location."

"Wife's family lived in house, husband's family moved in. Kids moving in feel they are imposing. Kids already there feel imposed upon."

### Rivalry over Friends

"There is a problem with friends accepting the stepbrother or sister and the problem of how to find time with friends and not stepsiblings."

### Rivalry over Stepgrandparental affection

"My sons have no relatives nearby and feel hurt that their stepgrandmother does not pay as much attention to them as her own grandchildren, nor does she acknowledge their birthdays. My mother, however, treats my stepdaughter as fairly as her own grandchildren and has always remembered birthdays, Christmas, etc. This conflict leaves a lot of bad feelings."

"Not major, but grandparents have continued to show considerable favoritism toward their biological grandchildren."

### Rivalry over Chores

"The girl feels she's required to do more chores while stepbrother does less, and real brother (younger) does even less!"

We can see, now, how deep are the emotions involved in stepsibling rivalry. Does this mean that all stepsibling relations are constantly marked by tumultuous competition? Or do they have ways of producing outcomes that make stepfamily continuity possible and enhance children's development? What, in short, are the positive patterns of adaptation that result from the dynamics of stepsibling rivalry?

Two potentially beneficial outcomes may emerge from these stepsibling tensions: 1. Rivalry can be usefully channeled into the processes whereby a child establishes his identity; 2. Rivalry can also produce stepsibling coalitions and solidarities. These possibilities are not mutually exclusive; they may overlap in the same relationships, and may be shown by different persons in the same stepfamily.

### The Cain Complex: Finding Out Who You are by Learning Who You are Not

When people grow up, they come to establish who they are by imitating significant people in their lives. In earlier childhood, the same-sex parent is used as a model for defining oneself in basic ways. As one gets older, the sample from which one chooses models gets wider, to include peers, siblings, and teachers. This process of defining ourselves by adopting traits of other people is called *identification*.

Identification does not consist solely in imitating the other person's behavior. It leads to the establishment of a child's identity—his sense of self—because he comes to internalize the behavior and see the characteristics that produce the behavior as somehow part of himself. This process is not necessarily inspired by feelings of unmixed fondness for the person used as a model.[6] Identification does not cease at the end of childhood, because our self-definition is continuous, even though in adulthood our imitation of some aspects of others' characteristics does not as fundamentally alter who we are. Even so, "identity crises" are not unknown among young adults.[7]

Identification with a sibling takes place in an emotional atmosphere tinged with competition and rivalry. As with parent-centered identification, it is not simply based on admiration or adulation; it can be inspired by animosity and envy. A child may attempt to model his or her behavior on that of another sibling in order to win out in some aspect of the contest between them for parental esteem or peer approval.

The same backdrop of competition can also produce a pattern of behavior that at first sight appears to be the opposite of identification. A child may define who he is by deliberately picking out the characteristics of another significant person in his life and defining himself as different or opposite in that regard. In this case a sibling is chosen as a negative model, an example against which a child defines himself. This process of finding out who you are by finding out who you are not is called *deidentification*. This, too, is an adaptation to rivalry. It usually takes place by the age of six, and is a "defensive maneuver" against the emotional pressure of rivalry with a sibling. The intensity of competition is lessened when a child pretends to himself that he does not want to be like his competitor in any way.[8]

One study showed that deidentification was most likely between oldest siblings and the next one in line. The lowest likelihood was shown by pairs of siblings who were separated by age from one another by another sibling. In other words, the intensity of the feeling with which the deidentification coped was not very high between, say, an oldest and a youngest, while it was highest between the oldest and the next one in line.

The researchers also found that the negative modeling was stronger between children of the same sex. As noted above, the same appears to be true for sibling rivalry. Boys will feel more competition with other boys, and girls with girls, because the two sexes have different measures of competency; rivalry with someone whose proofs of excellence are different is less likely. By the same token, discovering who one is by choosing a comparable person to be deliberately different from is more probable between children of the same sex, because then the grounds for comparison have more meaning.[9] The authors conclude that ". . . the results support the psychoanalytic formulation that de-identification is a mechanism for resolving sibling rivalry, a *Cain Complex*."[10] Just as Cain and Abel were brothers and yet different—herdsman and husbandman—deidentification establishes identities by differentiating between siblings in intense competition.

Thus identification and deidentification both take place in the context of sibling rivalry. In both cases another youngster is used as a guide to self-definition, either in a positive or a negative sense. Both are adaptations that can appear between stepsiblings.

The cases described at the beginning of this chapter show the two patterns; each has had different outcomes. Brenda Goldberg's account describes a situation of very intense competition, as we would expect, between stepsiblings of the same sex. Frederick was the oldest in the family, and in spite of having spent a lot of time in boarding school, probably was in a preeminent position with his mother after her divorce. There is no mention of his reaction to the arrival of his stepfather, who dislodged him from the role of oldest male, because this was not the focus of the research; nonetheless, we can surmise that at least part of his hostility toward his stepsiblings came from his stepfather's having deprived him of preeminence with his mother. He was also obliged to resume the role of a child, losing his quasi-adult status. But he had considerable power, because he remained the oldest and because he was often left in charge by his mother and stepfather.

Frederick was both angry and powerful; the picture Brenda paints of his tyranny is stark. His main victim was Victor, who was a potential competitor because he was the only other male child and because he was obliged to share his room with him, but easily beaten because he was small and "funny looking." Not surprisingly, Victor became a sort of slave of Frederick, making his bed, and being manipulated in ploys against the other youngsters in the family. Victor, for his part, had no choice but to capitulate. Not only did he surrender, but Brenda mentions that now Victor is most like Frederick. "Identification with the aggressor" appears to have been Victor's method of adaptation to oppression by his stepbrother. His bleak choice was really no choice at all.

Brenda's own adaptation is more complicated, but had a similar outcome. Brenda had little in the way of a mother's love, because even before her parents were divorced, her mother was going insane and was often out of touch with reality. In the stepfamily, however, she was confronted by a stepmother who clearly favored her own children over Brenda and her brother and sister. Brenda remembers that her own brother and sister were physically beaten and her stepmother's children were not; whether this is literally true or not is less important than that it is her recollection.

To compound the feeling of deprivation, Brenda's stepsiblings had a generous father in California whose largesse at Christmas was overwhelming. Note that in her account, Brenda talks of a "*huge* box of presents," "with 20 million presents in it." These are the recollections of a woman in her mid-twenties, who still feels the pain of losing out in her competition, not simply because the presents are desirable in themselves, but because they underline the lack of equity between the biological siblings and the stepsiblings. The stepsiblings have a parent somewhere else, one who is bountiful and kind. But Brenda and her siblings have only an insane mother who provides nothing.

This stepfamily started for Brenda when she was a pre-adolescent, and she lived through her teens while adapting to it. This required her to fill two very tall orders: she had to join in a new family, with its extraordinarily complicated patterns, and one in which she was clearly on the losing side in stepsibling competition. At the same time she had to accomplish all the adaptive tasks of adolescence, not only undergoing the physical changes of puberty, but the even more difficult job of finding out who she was. All the while, she had to prepare eventually to leave the very same family she was striving to join.

Brenda's solution was to try to be like Felicity. In one way, this was similar to the adaptation of her brother Victor, although Felicity was not, apparently, as much of an aggressor as Frederick was. But Brenda and Felicity were more or less of the same age, and were of the same sex, so that the potential for competition was certainly very strong. The cards were stacked against Brenda because Felicity had a mother who favored her and a generous absent father, while Brenda had neither. Thus Brenda is still seeking to be like Felicity in her efforts to make her stepmother love her just as much. Therefore, just as Victor turned out to be like Frederick, Brenda is trying to be like Felicity.

Of course, this use of identification as an escape hatch from stepsibling rivalry is not likely to succeed. Brenda's stepmother will never love her as much as her stepsister, and as long as she holds on to this dream, Brenda will have difficulty in achieving autonomy. While Brenda's quest may not be *logical* in the sense of pure rationality, it is *psycho-logical,* because although futile, it is understandable, given the structure of the stepsibling relationships in the Goldberg family.

While the case of Brenda and her stepsiblings shows how intense competition can produce an ambivalent type of identification, Pete Gilbert and his stepbrother show a significantly different pattern. A set of fairly stable step-relationships seems to have emerged in spite of the tempestuous teens of Pete and Max. The Gilbert family may have survived at least in part because the destructive hostility between the boys was harnessed in a way that seems to have benefitted both of them.

They started out as bitter rivals, having to share a place of privilege that essentially cannot be shared—that of being the youngest in a fairly large brood of siblings. Although Max was not interviewed, one suspects that it must have been particularly difficult for him, since he was taken care of by his mother for years, and because Pete had an older sibling who could support him in his warfare. The boys also had to share a place of privacy—their bedroom. It is impossible to tell for whom this was harder; for Pete, whose personal space was being encroached upon, or Max, who was constantly made to feel like an outsider by his stepbrother. And above all, these wrenching changes confronted the boys in early adolescence, when the job of seeking an identity, of learning how to define oneself, seems pressing and sometimes overwhelming.

What emerges from Pete's recollections is a distinct process, in which each boy carefully carved out an identity for himself that was similar enough to be comparable to that of his stepbrother, but different enough to be unique. For instance, with regard to high school sports, Pete claimed, "there was never any competition between us in track. I didn't avoid it [his stepbrother's event] deliberately. I do what I want to do." The other patterns of mutual differentiations, however, suggest that Pete's decisions were not as free as he remembers them to be.

In their tastes in dating, girls, and music, for instance, they were comparable but different. With regard to dating, when one was monogamous, the other was a social butterfly; when the monogamous one began ranging farther afield, the other became monogamous. One likes girls with a particular sort of build, and the other likes girls with an obviously different build. Both like music, but carefully differentiate their likes from the other's. It is as if each is carefully and constantly watching the other, making certain that the grounds for comparison are close enough to make differences noticeable.

Stepsibling deidentification thus requires that people be fairly similar for them to be able to establish their distinctiveness. When one is searching to find out who one is, it is helpful to have a clear idea who one is not. Pete and Max may never be friendly with one another, but their mutual debt is large, because it was their very rivalry that helped them to find out who they are. Pete and Max Gilbert are successful examples of taking the potentially destructive hostility between intensely competitive stepsiblings and channeling it in a developmentally useful direction.

The cases of Pete and Brenda both involved intense stepsibling rivalry. Although they may seem contradictory, Pete and Brenda show how stepsibling identification and deidentification may both be mechanisms for defusing the tensions. One involves stepbrothers defining themselves as scrupulously distinct from one another. The other involves one stepsister forlornly imitating her counterpart in a search for her stepmother's love.

Identification and deidentification are not the only outcomes of stepsibling rivalry. One other possible reaction is the formation of coalitions. The next case study illustrates this process.

### Stepsibling Solidarity: The Case of Golda Cohen

Golda Cohen grew up in a complex stepfamily. Her mother and father were also parents to her brothers, Brian and Dave, and her sister, Frieda. There were half-siblings as well. Her father was a widower who brought his daughters Leah and Marilyn, Golda's half-sisters, into the family. Her mother had been divorced and brought in her daughter, Pearl. Leah and Marilyn, of course, were stepsisters of Pearl. Marilyn, born in 1917, is the oldest; Leah was born the next year, and Pearl the next. The mutual children appeared when the others were around ten years old: Golda in 1928, Frieda in 1930, Brian in 1932, and Dave in 1938. Thus, while the seven youngsters were growing up together there two distinct age sets: Marilyn and Leah, who were stepsisters to Pearl on the one hand, and the new babies Golda, Brian, Dave, and Frieda on the other.

Golda remembers it as a family in which there was a great deal of conflict. "We were brought up in a house with a lot of strife. They were always screaming and fighting. I was just brought up with screaming and fighting as a way of life. . .We're not an affectionate family—there was never any kissing or hugging or 'I love yous.' " Her father was emotionally unavailable. "My father was always—he was a father, but he went to work and brought in the money and disappeared. He wasn't an affectionate type of person at all. He was a father, but he was never there."

Her early relationship with her younger sister Frieda was one of normal competition. "I didn't really feel closer to Freida because we were the same age—practically—we're two years apart and we fought over boyfriends, you know, the whole thing. . ."

Her relations with her half-sisters were fairly distant at the beginning, but seem to have gotten mellower as time passed:

> Pearl got married when she was about sixteen, so I was very young when she left the house but we kept in contact. She seems to be closer to us. . . .there's more of a distance with the others. She's the one that initiates, makes all the phone calls, constantly calling us. She calls her half-sisters Marilyn and Leah regularly. She keeps begging Leah to come visit her, because Leah had never got married and *we all feel responsible for Leah so we all keep in touch.* You know, she lives by herself and she's the only one who had never gotten married so *we all are protective of her.* [emphasis added]

The half-sisters, sisters, and stepsisters have become closer now that they are middle-aged. At present, three of them live within a block of each other and maintain regular contact. Part of the mid-life cohesion between Golda, Frieda, and their half-sisters may also be traceable to the fact that their parents were distant, and to the fact that the stepsisters serve as parent substitutes. "It was almost as if I was brought up with three mothers rather than sisters. Leah and Pearl were the ones who took care of me when I was little—they were babysitting for me all the time—my mother worked until Dave was born."

As for the boys, they have not stayed close to their half-sisters.

> The boys seemed to have drifted off. . .My brother Dave, I'm the only one in the family that will bother with him—he went off—they are all angry at him because he's a non-believer, and when my mother died he walked out right after the funeral. He wouldn't sit shiva. [the Jewish mourning period] Dave was the baby of the family, my mother really babied him, and I think he tried to get away from all that, and he was trying to find himself for a long time."

Brian and Dave are hostile to each other, as well, deliberately avoiding one another.

Golda says that as she and her sister and half-sisters have gotten older, they have developed a strong and supportive network.

> I think as we became adults, as the parents died off, I think that we had to depend on each other. . .I was close to Pearl [a half-sister] and Frieda [a sister] as I was growing and I became closer to Leah [another half-sister] only recently since we began to talk and find more things in common. But she was always older than me.

In some ways, her relationship with her half-sister Leah is stronger than with her sister Frieda:

> You know, suddenly the age difference has disappeared and I find that I can talk to her and get deeper conversations because Frieda is very shallow to talk to. I learned through a lot of other things in living and a little therapy to open up. And when I opened up, Leah was the one who was receptive and Frieda doesn't understand. She looks at me blankly like she doesn't know what I'm talking about. [Nowadays, if I had a personal problem,] I think I would talk to Leah more than anyone else because I think she would be more understanding.

While at times stepsibling relations will remain in hostile camps based on blood, other types of alliances between youngsters can emerge on the basis of loyalties that can be as powerful. Two are particularly strong potential bases: sex and age. One or the other of these can be effective bases of tactical alliances. An early coalition between children who are of the same age and of the same sex may be less likely, because the double similarity may be more likely to lead to increased competition rather than coalition. But as people grow into adulthood, age differences become less important. As the phases of their lives become more similar, networks of mutual dependence can emerge, particularly between stepsiblings and half-siblings of the same sex.

Strictly speaking, Golda Cohen herself is a half-sibling. But the network of mutual support in which she lives and which she describes is one between same-sex stepsisters. Although Golda herself is linked to them by blood, her half-sisters are not so linked to each other. Her descriptions have therefore been used to illustrate stepsibling solidarity. Thus stepfamilies should not be seen as simply a scene of trench warfare between youngsters but where the possibility of love and support can emerge, particularly after the heat of initial competition has faded.

In nuclear families, brothers and sisters support one another, too, in addition to competing with each other. Several studies have been made of supportive relations between siblings. In general, the findings are that biological "sibling solidarity" is more prevalent in working-class than in middle-class families, that it is marked by cordial but not intense relations, and that the most important aspect of these positive feelings is that they grew out of siblings' personal choices, rather than being forced by parents during childhood. Golda Cohen's stepsibling solidarity seems to fit each of these characteristics, and we can tentatively conclude that stepsibling solidarity probably has the same sorts of dynamics as sibling solidarity.[11]

### Patterns and Problems of Stepsibling Rivalry: A Summary

The recurring tensions of stepsibling rivalry can be summed up in three general rubrics. The first can be called "Equality is Not Enough," and revolves around stepsiblings and the problem of legitimacy and the scarcity of love. The second, "Invaders and Landlords," is produced by the problem of scarce space. Finally, there is the "Santa Claus Syndrome," whereby absent biological parents serve to upset the balance of stepsibling competition. Some of the outcomes can be negative. But there are redeeming aspects of stepsibling life—identification, de-identification, and stepsibling coalitions. By way of conclusion to this chapter, let us sum up these rubrics.

### Equality is Not Enough

Parents often attempt to solve the problem of sibling rivalry by being evenhanded, observing scrupulous equality. Competition for parental affection can be somewhat stabilized by convincing youngsters that love and its symbols are equitably distributed. This pattern poses problems for a stepfamily.

First, it presents serious loyalty conflicts for biological parents. It requires a parent to surrender the powerful attachment felt for biological children and to treat stepchildren equally. Though logical, this course is extremely difficult for a parent to follow because it is so emotionally wrenching. Thus though absolute equity may seem to be an answer to stepsibling rivalry, it is less likely than clear partiality of biological parents for their offspring. Hence the conventional tactic that is used in reducing intersibling tensions is much more difficult to follow in the stepfamily.

Second, even if it were possible for stepparents to impose a strictly egalitarian regime, such a solution will not necessarily be satisfactory to stepsiblings. Siblings may resent one another, but all have the same presumptive claim to a parent's love, because all are related by blood. Real and imagined gradations derived from age-order and sex notwithstanding, all biological siblings share an essentially equal claim their parents. Not so stepsiblings. It is nearly impossible for stepsiblings to see one another as having the same right to scarce resources. A child can hardly perceive a stepsibling as having the same right to his parent's love and its symbols as the child himself has. Unless a set of stepsiblings are joined in a stepfamily at a very early age, before exclusive claims to the biological parent's love are felt, the solution of equity between stepsiblings will be no solution at all. Equality between stepsiblings is not enough, because they do not consider one another's claims to have equal legitimacy. This is the central problem in stepsibling rivalry.

## Invaders and Landlords

Unless a newly formed stepfamily moves to new, neutral ground when it is formed, it is almost inevitable that, at the beginning, at least, there will be tensions flowing from sharing of space. If one side of the stepfamily moves into the habitual residence of the other, the incoming group will be seen as invaders, by the indigenous members and perhaps by themselves as well. The newcomers will see their counterparts as asserting a proprietary claim to living space, never feeling at home precisely where they should expect to feel at home. In such a situation, neither the newcomers nor their hosts will be comfortable.

One of the respondents provided a stark illustration of the degree of forced intimacy stepsiblinghood can involve:

Growing up, there was a lot of resentment because I hated sharing a bed with them [her stepsiblings]. One of the jokes (that you say are jokes because a lot of truth is in it) I said was 'I got married so I could have a bed of my own.' Because I never remembered having a bed of my own when I lived at home. In fact I remember there was a time when we were three or four of us in a bed. . . .We all had to share one big double bed.

Less extreme was the account of another respondent about the arrival of her stepsiblings. "I felt as if I was always entertaining guests. I mean, 'Are they ever going to go home?'" She originally had her own room in the house, but when her father remarried, her stepmother (in a misdirected effort to produce equality) insisted she share a room with her stepsisters. "There was no reason for me to leave my room. They took me out of my room and put me in with them."

### The Santa Claus Syndrome

The laws of chance make it unlikely that a remarriage will take place between people of precisely the same income group or occupational category. Even when stepfamilies are formed by merging partners of approximately the same social background, grandparents and the prosperity (or lack thereof) of ex-spouses make for uneven distributions of wealth within the stepfamily and in its surrounding kin.

This is a practical problem for stepparents, because the peculiar legal status of the stepfamily means that a substantial contribution to the family's finances may come, at least in theory, from someone outside. Suppose one set of stepsiblings has a noncustodial parent who is wealthier than the children's stepparent. In such a situation, unless they are willing to let the stepsiblings have unequal wealth, the adults might make an effort to evenly distribute child-support payments so that all the youngsters share their benefits equally. If they do this, however, they may be in technical violation of the law, since these payments are supposedly for one set of children and not the other.

While the children are young, it is more likely that they will experience conflict based on the generosity of absent parents and/or grandparents in the form of jealousy over presents. Brenda Goldberg's recollections of the big box of presents for her stepsiblings at Christmas is ample illustration of this. But issues of wealth in the meta-family do not fade among older stepsiblings. One respondent said, "[My stepsisters] had a very rich uncle. Their mother's brother. He set [her stepsister's] husband up in business, and she did very well. . .And many times I was a little jealous of that."

*The Benefits of Stepsibling Living: Identification, Deidentification, and Solidarity*

Much of the foregoing has stressed the sources of tension between stepsiblings; this may have produced the impression that stepsibling rivalry is an inescapable mire of hostility. Although there are pitfalls, there are distinct benefits as well. Pete Gilbert and Brenda Goldberg found out who they are with the aid of stepsiblings. For all the problems she faced, Brenda's experiences were enriched by having Felicity there; remember that Brenda said, "Felicity is a play-type sister. Joan is a sister-sister." Although Pete overtly felt disdain for Max, the two boys always chose activities similar enough so that they could measure themselves against one another. And, after all, Pete could "hate" Max, as his friend pointed out; this was an advantage of being a stepbrother.

Stepsiblings, therefore, present expanded opportunities for children, a larger range of choices to imitate or be different from than blood siblings. Since there is less of a family tie, the relationship is less pressured, less encumbered by feelings of obligation based on blood. Wallerstein and Kelly provide a perceptive description:

> Several children approved of their new siblings and felt that the losses associated with the divorce had been more than balanced by the acquisition of new stepsiblings. Tom, aged twelve, commented, 'Kids have an easier time with divorce that grownups. They get something—a stepmom or a stepdad, more sisters and more brothers.'[12]

An additional advantage was shown by the mutual support of Golda Cohen and her stepsisters and half-sisters. As one commentator has said:

> As time passes, don't be surprised to discover new alliances being formed between stepsiblings. Some may actually seem to exclude natural brothers and sisters. In one instance I observed a thirteen-year-old girl who was always in relentless competition with her sixteen-year-old-sister whom she mistakenly believed her mother favored. When her mother remarried, she quickly developed a strong friendship with her eighteen-year-old stepsister. They had more in common than she had with her own sister. She felt appreciated and understood; her conflicts with her own sister gradually diminished.[13]

In short, coalitions can form between stepsiblings. Sometimes these are based on similar life stages; once again, a stepsister or stepbrother is a more emotionally neutral person from whom to obtain information about the opposite sex or about how to act. Warm, supportive coalitions can also form between same-sex stepsiblings, particularly later in life, when age differences become less important. But they need not be based on closeness in age—one stepchild can act "parental" to another, or serve as a "big brother" or "big sister" to emulate.

The sources of stepsibling tension revolve around parental equity, space, and class. Their outcomes can include pseudomutuality and detachment, but can also include constructive identification, deidentification, and stepsibling solidarity. Which of these patterns emerges and becomes dominant depends greatly on factors such as stepfamily awareness and willingness to cope with novel situations. It is thus difficult to state in any systematic way what the outcomes will be in any particular family. Such predictions cannot as yet be made, in the absence of large-scale research into stepsibling relations.

In all of the foregoing, stepsibling competition arises over resources that may be scarce but (at least in theory) can be divided equally. When sets of stepsiblings are merged, however, what transpires is a sudden redistribution of certain other resources that by definition cannot be distributed equally: the family power and prestige attached to children's birth order and age order. Rivalry over these coveted items requires a separate discussion.

## Notes

1. Ruth Roosevelt and Jeanette Lofas, *Living in Step* (New York: Stein and Day, 1976), p. 149.
2. Einstein, 1973, *The Stepfamily*, p. 111.
3. Ibid., p. 297.
4. Brenda Bryant, "Sibling Relationships in Middle Childhood," Lamb & Sutton-Smith, eds., 1982, *Sibling Relationships*, pp. 87–121.
5. Helgola Ross and Joel Milgram "Important Variables in Adult Sibling Relationships: A Qualitative Study," in Lamb and Sutton-Smith, 1982, *Sibling Relationships*, pp. 225–49.
6. See Walter Mischel, "Sex Typing and Socialization," *Manual of Child Psychology*, Vol. II, ed. Paul Mussen (New York: Wiley, 1970), pp. 18–19.
7. Erik Erikson, Childhood and Society (New York: Norton, 1963), pp. 306–25.
8. Brenda Bryant, "Middle Childhood," p. 96.
9. Frances Schachter et al. "Sibling Deidentification," *Developmental Psychology* 12 (September 1976):418–27.
10. Ibid., p. 427. Emphasis added.
11. Elaine Cumming and David Schneider, "Sibling Solidarity: A Property of American Kinship," *American Anthropologist* 63 (March 1961):498–507; George Rosenberg and Donald Anspach, "Sibling Solidarity in the Working Class," *Journal of Marriage and the Family* 35 (February 1983):108–13;

Graham Allan, "Sibling Solidarity," *Journal of Marriage and the Family* 39 (February 1977):177–84.

12. Judith Wallerstein and Joan Kelly, *Surviving the Breakup: How Children and Parents Cope with Divorce* (New York: Basic Books, 1980), p. 298.

13. Frederick Flach, "Now You Have a New Brother and Sister," *Remarriage* (May, 1985):20.

# 3

# Revolution in the Ranks: Changes in Birth Order and Age Order

*Now Israel loved Joseph more than any other of his children, because he was the son of his old age; and he made him a long robe with sleeves. But when his brothers saw that their father loved him more than all his brothers, they hated him, and could not speak peaceably to him.*
—Genesis 37: 3–4

Adult society has different degrees of inequality based on wealth, power, prestige—whatever is scarce that adults value highly. The social world of children is divided into layers of a different sort. One of the most important is that of age. If adults have class and status rankings, siblings have a hierarchy based on the order in which children were born. Differences in age that seem negligible for grownups have great significance for youngsters, particularly those in the same family. What is more, the age interval between children can affect the way in which they play together or whether they play together at all.

Stepfamilies in which children are combined from one or more previous marriages of both spouses present some unusual problems of adjustment in the sibling pecking order. In the intact nuclear family, the order in which children are born fixes their place in the age order of their brothers and sisters; the order of children's birth simply determines what their order of age is. The age interval between siblings is also fixed by the order in which they are born; the *distance* in age between a child and other siblings is simply a function of when he was born. In a phrase, birth order, age order, and birth interval are all fixed statuses. This provides a relatively stable (if potentially oppressive) ranking system for children.

In the combination stepfamily, though, the three factors are not necessarily fixed. When sets of siblings are combined, the order in which a person has been born is not necessarily the same as the place a child holds in the overall age order of the children in the stepfamily. The number of years between a child and his next-oldest or next-youngest sibling is not the same as the number of years between him and the next-oldest or next-youngest child in the stepfamily. In short, age order is not determined by birth order; age interval in the stepsibling hierarchy is not determined by birth interval.

Thus the struggle for dominance in the children's power structure is a special case of stepsibling rivalry, because the power deriving from a particular rank in the age hierarchy is a scarce resource over which there is competition. It is treated separately here not only because it seems less tractable, but because there has been so much speculation and debate among social scientists over what effects, if any, such rankings have on children's development.

### Sibling Pecking Orders

*Robert (11):* I have to say off the top of my head that I wish my brother was never born, because the state I'm in now, I'm affection-starved, and I would love to have all the attention I used to have when I was an only child. My point of view is that, no matter how much older you are, if you're older you get more responsibilities because the parents feel you're more mentally developed. Even if we were twins and I was a half-hour older, I'd be getting more responsibilities!

*Nate (13):* I don't like being the middle kid cause you get all the disadvantages. If you do something to your sister or brother you get in trouble, and if they do something to you, you *still* get in trouble. I don't like to get caught in the middle of everything.

*Annie (10):* There are some advantages to being the youngest, I guess. My older brother and sister get the big punishments. . . . Being the youngest is easier than being in the middle or the oldest—basically because nothing can be done about it![1]

There is an old and continuing debate among social scientists about whether birth order, age order and age interval have any effects upon children's development, and, if so, just what those effects are. As early as 1874, Galton's "responsibility model" suggested that being the first born conferred a special status among children in a family. But subsequent research has shown inconsistent results, mostly because of a certain confusion over the importance of age order and age interval.

At first, it was thought that there was a relation between delinquency and age order.[2] The position of the oldest, or first-born, child was also found to be problematic in one sociometric study. When children were asked for spontaneous choices of who they prefered to be with, the youngest almost always was chosen as most desirable, and the oldest among those designated as least desirable. There seems to be a strong pattern of rejection between the first-born child and the next in line.[3]

Schachter's research also indicates the effects of being the oldest for females. The "anxiety affiliation model" argues that "in states of anxiety first-born females were more likely to seek the company and valuation of others than were later-born females who were more likely to seek isolation. . . ."[4]

An elaborate description of the personality types that develop from birth order and age order was provided by Bossard and Boll. They suggest that first-born children develop capacities for leadership, as evidenced by the prevalence of first-born children among listings in *Who's Who:* ". . . the oldest child is generally 'on the spot,' as is the leader of any group, to perform a little better and to act a little more circumspectly than his younger followers."[5] Middle children are in competition with older children and manifest sadism or defeatism with regard to younger children; an inordinate number of "restless neurotics" are middle children. Finally, there is the baby, for whom the jealousy of older siblings leads to his exploitation of his babyhood and/or a desire to outdo his older brothers and sisters. These authors also propose typical personality outcomes for siblings in large families. As in small families, the first born is in a responsible, policeman-like role, the second agreeable and sociable, the third socially ambitious, the fourth studious and scholarly, the fifth an isolate, the sixth sickly, and the last a baby and/or a "bad" child. Bossard and Boll also suggest that the age interval of siblings is important in that to the extent that birth order is important in how siblings interact these effects will be intensified by the children being close in age, and diminished insofar as they are distant in age.

The effect of large numbers of siblings is looked at in combination with that of age interval by Zajonc, who suggests that the intelligence of a child is diminished in proportion to the number of children in the family, but that this is mitigated to the extent that the other children are older. This so-called *confluence model* holds that the rapidity of a child's development is retarded to the degree that he interacts with children close in age rather than adults; the most rapid and mature development would be accomplished by an only child. Somewhat slower would be a child with a sibling who was considerably older and hence "more adult," while the slowest would be shown by a child with many siblings close to him in age.[6]

Recently, though, it has been suggested that birth order in itself only accounts for a small amount of the differences in children's intelligence,[7] and that age interval explains little more. Another study argues that new data show there is little effect of sibling spacing on children.[8]

Finally, a very recent study shows that birth order indeed has little effect on children's academic achievement, but that it does have a strong effect on children's later success in social relationships, even when number of siblings, age, sex, and family income are held constant.[9]

On balance, it appears that birth order, age order, and birth interval seem to have some effect on children in biological families, although the effects of these factors have not been precisely assessed. The clearest picture that emerges is that of the importance of being the first born. This position is held by a child who by definition was an only child until his younger sibling came along, depriving him of a previously held monopoly on parental affection and attention. The oldest child also has greater responsibilities, by dint of his comparatively advanced development. He also has greater freedom and power, which may not neatly counterbalance the difficulties of the role, but may provide some compensation.

A few observations have been made by others with regard to change in these roles when children are joined in a stepfamily. Duberman, for instance, observed that in biological families, the first-born child frequently feels rejected, inferior, jealous, and competitive when a sibling is born. In combination stepfamilies, there are two first-born children, doubling the probability and strength of these conflicts. In nuclear families, the first-born child, in time, learns to cope with these disruptive emotions and to adapt, and the same seems to be true among stepsiblings. Duberman found that 42 percent of her respondents asserted that the stepsiblings' relationships were getting better.[10]

On the basis of clinical work, Stuart and Jacobson point out that the first born bears the heaviest burden in a combination stepfamily. "The most difficult issue concerns the responsibilities and prerogatives of the eldest. . . . A loss in position as a parent's confidante following a parent's remarriage can be a very painful experience for a child."[11]

Some observers of the stepfamily disagree about the pattern of age-order adaptations. Linda Craven says that stepsiblings closer in age and of the same sex are more likely to be in conflict. Yet Wallerstein and Kelly say, ". . . children of both parents were likely to be closer in age and to form a subgroup within the family."[12]

By and large, other students of the stepfamily have paid scant attention to the problems attendant on merging age- and birth-hierarchies in stepfamilies. We therefore need primary sources. The survey of the

Stepfamily Association of America provides descriptions by parents who are observing the sibling power shifts firsthand.

## Patterns of Change

Five distinct patterns are possible when children are combined in a stepfamily: 1. an only child becomes the oldest child 2. an only child becomes the youngest child 3. an only child becomes a middle child 4. an oldest child becomes a middle child 5. a youngest child becomes a middle child. A less distinct shift is that a middle child can change location in the hierarchy. In the first three patterns, a child goes from having been the center of parental attention to sharing the role of son or daughter with others who are not his blood relatives; he has gone from a solo act to one where he is on stage with a company of players. In the fourth pattern, a child who was the youngest, and in many ways the center of attention, becomes one of a crowd—a prince or princess who has lost a throne. In the last case, the eldest child, who may have had the greatest responsibilities as well as the greatest power, also becomes one of the crowd; he is like a policeman who has lost his beat.

The accounts of the parents who responded to the survey provided descriptions of the reactions of their children who underwent these role transformations typical of the combination stepfamily. It would be a mistake to generalize too much, but the descriptions can be put together into a tentative picture of combination stepfamily processes.

## From Solo to Group Living

*An only child becomes the oldest child:*

"She's almost a mother hen to the stepbrothers and stepsister. She's learned a lot of responsibility."

*An only child becomes the youngest child:*

"Resentful of shared attention, attempted to emulate and demand the same privileges as the older stepsiblings."

*An only child becomes a middle child:*

"My stepdaughter greatly resented having to share in all aspects of our new family. She had and still has a lot of problems communicating with other family members."

"The only child felt a big loss of both time and a family structure she was familiar with. She still feels that, after five years in the new family."

There is a fourth possibility. In this family, two only children were combined so that one became oldest and the other became youngest, sixteen years old and seven years old, respectively. The mother wrote:

> I feel they both like having a brother. When one is gone, the other gets a little lonely or bored. I think the younger child gets on the older young man's nerves sometimes. The older one needs his privacy, more so than the younger one. I feel it is very important to keep the love, attention, discipline and caring even between them at all times. They are close, but I don't feel they will be as close as real brothers. We may have another child [half-sibling] and I feel they both would enjoy it. They were both the only children in the previous families. I think they like having each other instead of still being the only child.

We can speculate that for an only child to become an oldest child may on balance may be a positive experience, because both are positions of privilege. There is the possibility, of course, that this child will be given *too much* responsibility, as in the case of Brenda Goldberg's stepbrother, Frederick. For an only child to become a youngest child is more difficult; being the "baby" has certain advantages, but that status does not have enough power or privilege to offset the loss of the monopoly possessed by an only child. And for an only child to become a middle child may be the most difficult of the three, since the loss of the monopoly is not offset by the special status of being the youngest or oldest; such a child is most likely to feel lost in the shuffle. In the case of the fourth possibility, the children have probably made the best sort of accommodation that can be expected under the circumstances: they both still have a special status—youngest or oldest—but have the company and companionship they missed when they were only children.

### The "Prince" Loses His Throne

"At twenty-one, my daughter (already married) had an intense bout with jealousy—probably combined with homesickness, since she's in Germany with her husband."

"[My son] scapegoated the younger stepsibling whenever possible. This is a boy who is now flanked by girls on both sides."

"I think that the formerly youngest child has mixed feelings about having an instant younger brother. While I believe he likes the idea of no longer being the youngest, he realizes that this new position has its share of grief, since his younger brother wants to be just like him, and not only imitates him but follows him around, rarely leaving him in peace.''

"She was a girl with four boys. It didn't change life too much."

"The youngest became a middle child, but tried to remain the youngest for two years, but then outgrew this in her late teens."

In addition to the SAA survey, the author conducted a group interview on the issue of age order with a group of stepsiblings in combination stepfamilies. One of the questions asked was, "How do you feel about changing from being the youngest to a middle child?" And the answers were as follows:

"I got to boss another person."

"I liked being the youngest because I got a lot of attention. I liked it better when I was youngest."

"Now I'm not getting all the attention any more. It's like I'd rather have all the attention because I get blamed for everything now."

"Everyone picks on the youngest. You get more attention, [when you are the youngest] whether you like it or not."

"I'm still my mother's youngest, so I'm sort of youngest."

"I'm the oldest on my mother's side."

These two sets of answers suggest some tentative conclusions about the experience of going from youngest to middle child. Loss of status as youngest seems very difficult to accept. Most grievous is the loss of attention. The feeling of deprivation appears, in some cases, to persist into adulthood. Escape from the focus of attention may be welcome in some cases, when too much attention is a burden. Other compensations include the acquisition of power over someone younger and being a model for a younger child. All these effects may to some degree be modified by the different sexes of the children. The loss of the privilege attached to being the youngest may be offset by remaining the only girl amongst boys or the only boy amongst girls.

A significant way of preserving special status also seems to be that a child can hold onto the realization that he or she may not be the youngest in this stepfamily, but is still the youngest of the biological siblings.

### The Policeman Loses His Beat

"Pressure has been taken off. He wasn't as resentful as we thought he would be."

"It was difficult for him. He was de-roled and lost status (in retrospect) with his younger siblings who really liked and admired the two new older stepbrothers. He, however, has adjusted and is friends with the stepbrothers: he moved in with the other set of parents, as he did not do well here."

"This, I don't think, was a major problem for my son—much more of a problem was his having to deal with a stepfather. We were never really able to 'jell' in the sense of the oldest son (my stepson) having *very* serious emotional problems, which kept him from being included. . . ."

"Rather well. But he tells his natural father that his stepsisters are a 'pain' sometimes. It never made sense until now that he would have some resentment at being 'pushed' out of being first in line in birth order."

"My twins were no longer the 'oldest' but perhaps since this had always been a shared designation, it did not seem to have had much impact."

"This applied when my husband first married. However, the situation changed when my husband's oldest son moved out two years later. This question is hard for me to answer. I think it might have been difficult for my husband's oldest and my oldest to adjust because they began sharing a room together when my husband and I married. They had little in common, and therefore had their share of minor conflicts. They seem to get along better now that they don't have to deal with each other on a daily basis."

"He really rather got lost in the crowd. There were five kids and he really wasn't used to competing."

"My stepson, who was my husband's oldest, became the middle child between my daughters. He didn't seem to notice any change."

"Not too well. Skipping school, and under a counselor."

The picture that emerges from these descriptions is much less clear than with the other two patterns of revolution. There are reports that the adjustment was easy, and reports that there was so little adjustment that the sets of siblings never jelled. It may be that either the adaptation is so smooth as to be hardly noticeable, or it is so difficult that it hardly takes place at all. This may be because of factors that are operative in the other situations. If an oldest child of one sex becomes a middle child between children of another sex, it may be fairly painless. The preservation of oldest child status with a biological parent may help in an otherwise difficult loss of status. The oldest twins referred to may have had the easiest time, since they underwent the loss of status together, and were always the same age anyway.

The ambiguity of the descriptions might be traced back to the observations made by other researchers about the status of being the oldest in intact families. The eldest is in a position of privilege vis à vis the parents and of power vis à vis the other siblings. But this position has its drawbacks. By definition, the eldest is the first child that the parents have raised, and they are apt to make their mistakes with him or her and be most anxious and protective about him. Also, greater responsibility is placed on the eldest, and infractions of the rules are apt to be more severely punished, since an older child is expected to know better. Therefore, loss of status as eldest may not be unwelcome, when it is accompanied by being the only boy or girl, or when a child has a strong sense of being a biological parent's eldest. But when a policeman loses his beat and mitigating factors are not present, the loss can indeed be grievous.

The method used to study this situation has its limitations. Parents might not have a clear enough idea of how children are adapting. Since they want to see harmony and happiness, their responses to this questionnaire may not provide an entirely reliable report. These observations, therefore, must be taken as tentative.

### From Revolution to Resolution

This chapter has considered age-order changes in the stepfamily as a special case of stepsibling rivalry for two reasons. Age order is a source of power in children's ranking systems that cannot be distributed equitably; the only circumstance in which this is possible is for twins, and even then there may be one who is identified as first born. The outcomes to stepsibling rivalry discussed above cannot therefore always be applied to this kind of competition. There has also been much speculation, though little conclusive evidence, among family researchers that age-order places are important to children's development.

Little can be said about the long-term effects of changes in age order in combination stepfamilies. Research on this question has, as yet, not been done. And although it should be done, it is not within the scope of an introductory study such as this. It is possible that the results may be as ambiguous for stepsiblings as for siblings. A salient hypothesis is that having or losing first-born or oldest status is likely to be as important for stepsiblings as it seems to be for siblings.

The short-term effects of alterations in birth and age order and the role of age interval are unmistakeable. Although we cannot be sure if they are important in later life, we know that they are influential in the everyday operation of the stepfamily.

When such alterations involve a change from only child to living with another child or children, some changes are easier than others. Going from being an only child to oldest is apparently easiest, perhaps because both are positions of privilege. Changing from being only to youngest has benefits (being the "baby") and costs (no longer being on center stage), and may be thus somewhat less difficult. Going from only child to middle child is hardest, because a child can feel lost in the crowd, sandwiched in, when his or her previous experience is that of being the "only act in town."

Becoming a middle child when one was previously a youngest child has pluses and minuses. The minuses are that one is no longer the center of everyone's attention and able to get away with more as a result of being littlest. But the pluses include having a smaller person or persons to dominate, and being looked up to.

Losing the position of being the oldest to another child or children seems hardest of the three changes. But here again, there may be mitigating factors. If one is the only member of one's particular sex, one is still special in that way. It is hard to be a policeman always on the beat. Sometimes it is a relief to become a middle child, because that means that the pressure is off.

Just as these are patterns that emerge from the short-term effects of alterations in sibling age hierarchies, these tensions can be resolved in stepfamilies. Children adapt to changes in birth order, age order, and age intervals in ways that are not always distinct from their adaptations to stepsibling rivalry. Identification and deidentification are certainly strategies employed by siblings who have experienced such change. There may even be more extreme pathological reactions, such as those that might appear in any family in crisis. But there are ways of coping with this specific problem.

Except where the combinations of youngsters are made at a very early age, the children have to learn to "disaggregate" birth order, age order, and birth interval. They have to learn how to cope with the fact that while these things went together in the past, they do not in the present family. In learning to see the differences between the three orders, stepsiblings can see themselves as belonging to *parallel age hierarchies*. While age order may change after a child joins a combination stepfamily, his or her birth order, vis à vis the biological parents, does not. This adaptation is vital for a child's adjustment in a stepfamily, because it means adapting to an entirely new sibling social structure.

## Notes

1. Dorriet Kavanaugh, *Listen to Us! The Children's Express Report* (New York: Workman Publishing, 1978), pp. 49–52.
2. Cf. E. James Anthony, "The Behavior Disorders of Childhood," in Paul Mussen ed., *Manual of Child Psychology*, vol. II, (New York: Wiley, 1970) pp. 667–764; and Raymond Sletto, "Sibling Position and Juvenile Delinquency," *American Journal of Sociology* 39 (March 1934):657–69.
3. Paulette Cahn, "Sociometric Experiments on Groups of Siblings," *Sociometry* 15 (August–November 1952):306–10.
4. Brian Sutton-Smith, "Birth Order and Sibling Status Effects," in Lamb and Sutton-Smith, 1982, *Sibling Relationships*, pp. 153–65.
5. James Bossard, *The Sociology of Child Development* (New York: The Free Press, 1960), p. 103.
6. R.B. Zajonc, "Birth Order and Intellectual Development," *Psychological Review* 82 (January 1975):74–88; "The Birth Order Puzzle," *Journal of Personality and Social Psychology* 37 (August 1979):1325–41.
7. Sandra Scarr and Susan Grajek, "Similarities and Differences Among Siblings," in Lamb and Sutton-Smith, 1982, *Sibling Relationships*, pp. 357–81, esp. p. 371.
8. Richard Galbraith, "Sibling Spacing and Intellectual Development: A Closer Look at the Confluence Models," *Developmental Psychology* 18 (March 1982):151–73.
9. Lala Steelman and Brian Powell, "The Social and Academic Consequences of Birth Order: Real, Artificial, or Both?" *Journal of Marriage and the Family* 47 (February 1985):117–24.
10. Duberman, 1973, *Stepkin Relationships*, esp. p. 291.
11. Richard Stuart and Barbara Jacobson, *Second Marriage: Make It Happy, Make It Last* (New York: Norton, 1985), p. 194.
12. Linda Craven, *Stepfamilies: New Patterns in Harmony* (New York: Julian Messner, 1982); Judith Wallerstein and Joan Kelly, 1980, *Surviving the Breakup*, p. 296.

# 4

# Sex, Love, and Hostility: What Happens Between Opposite-Sex Stepsiblings?

> *Now Absalom, David's son, had a beautiful
> sister, whose name was Tamar; and after a
> time Amnon, David's son, loved her. And
> Amnon was so tormented that he made
> himself ill because of his sister Tamar; for she
> was a virgin, and it seemed impossible to
> Amnon to do anything to her.*
> —2 Samuel 13:1–2

### The Baums

The Baum family is a large stepfamily living in a suburb of Chicago. Robert and Elizabeth Baum had five children before Elizabeth died. Robert remarried three years after his first wife's death, to Priscilla Donovan, who had had two children before divorcing. Her ex-husband had moved to Texas and subsequently remarried, too, but died not long after. At the time of Robert and Priscilla's marriage, Robert's three oldest children had moved out to get married themselves. The Baum household's stepsiblings consisted of Priscilla's children and Robert's children. For five years or so, the important stepsibling interaction occurred between Gail and Christine Donovan, and Mary and William Baum. Priscilla and Robert also had a child of their own, Valerie, who was an infant during her half-siblings' adolescence and early adulthood.

William was in his late teens when this stepfamily began. Gail and Christine were pre-teenagers. A very close relationship between William and Gail developed, as Gail grew into and through puberty. William was handsome and athletic, and all the girls in the neighborhood had crushes on him. "I guess I could say I had a crush on him," admitted Gail, "but never thinking, like, anything would happen." For his part, William enjoyed the adulation of his youngest stepsibling, who was happy to be at his beck and call.

In describing her relationship with her brothers and stepbrother at the time, Gail said, "[Although they had moved out,] I always wanted my brothers to approve of who I dated, but William's approval meant more." To this day, William is jealous and protective, and Gail explains that "William feels responsible for me." Though William is in his late twenties and Gail in her early twenties, this could be construed as ordinary family closeness, except when the relationship is looked at a little more closely.

Gail's main emotional preoccupation, even now, is the affection of her stepfather, whom she calls her father. Her stepfather and her mother had a stormy relationship, to a great extent because of the latter's emotional problems. Perhaps because Gail perceived her mother as so destabilizing to the family, she became preoccupied with getting close to her stepfather and obtaining his affection. "I just felt he was right in so many ways. He gave her everything, but she was just sick, and she treated his kids unfairly." As it happened, Robert did adopt her and her stepsiblings, so that legally, he really is her father. Though Robert subsequently divorced Priscilla, he remains emotionally central in Gail's life. "If something happens to my father," she said in our interview, "what will I have?" At the time, she was twenty-four.

Robert remarried, to Joan, his present wife. What is significant is that Gail got married, too, at almost exactly the same time as her stepfather wed Joan. At the time, she was quite resentful of Joan and reproached her stepfather with statements such as, "You just don't care about my feelings." The interview after this point almost speaks for itself.

*Author:* "Why did you get married at that time?"

*Gail:* "I felt like, I've got to get out of this house. . . I felt like Joan didn't want me in the house. . . . [And then] I tried to stay married to prove to Robert that I was not like my mother."

With Robert as its main focus, her marriage, not surprisingly, did not last. William, too, had gotten married and he, too, got divorced. His marriage did not coincide with any significant event in the Baum-Donovan household, but his divorce coincided with the divorce of his stepsister, to whom he had come to feel a strong attraction.

*Author:* Do you feel superior to any of your siblings?

*Gail:* "I feel superior to *all* of them because I'm closest to my father [meaning her stepfather]. Mary used to say, 'I can't believe you told Robert, like, that you and your husband didn't make love the other night.' . . . I can tell him anything.''

*Author:* ''Who is better looking, of you and the other girls in the family?''

*Gail:* ''Mary.''

*Author:* ''Who does William think is better looking?''

*Gail:* ''Me [laughing]. He and Mary don't get along.''

*Author:* ''Are there any ways in which you feel they are superior to you?''

*Gail:* Only when I get down on myself. It sometimes makes me depressed to realize that Mary and William are Robert's real blood and I'm not.''

*Author:* ''Is there any likelihood of a sexual relationship developing between you and William?''

*Gail:* ''William *is* attracted to me. I get afraid. I wouldn't want to lose Robert. If people found out, they'd kill us. [William is jealous of her current boyfriend] William needs me, but I need somebody to think of me as a sister, not somebody to go to bed with.''

*Author:* It sounds as if sisterhood is more important than sex.

*Gail:* Yes, it is.

What sort of patterns can be seen in this tangled web of emotions? Gail felt an overwhelming need to join in as part of the Baum family, partly because of her awareness that her mother was cruel and capricious. This developed into an almost obsessive need for her stepfather's love. The need to be a Baum rather than a Donovan continues to this day, and her main concern is avoiding any condemnation in her stepfather's eyes. It appears that, at least to a certain extent, William is a substitute for Robert, since he is Robert's son. Gail and William see each other frequently, she is gratified by his attraction to her, yet she protects herself from any sexual relationship. Above all, Robert might find out, and this would, in her eyes, be catastrophic. William is now living his own life, lives with another woman with whom he has a stable relationship, and yet he, too, seems not to be able to establish his independence from the family.

Are the Baums typical? The safest thing to say would be that no stepfamily is typical. Yet this single stepfamily shows how the outcome of sexual attraction between stepsiblings can have far-reaching effects. It indicates that even the sexual magnetism that can occur between stepsiblings is not simple. For Gail, it is not simply a question of attraction to William, but of William as a substitute for Robert, her stepfather, to whom she is attached partly because of her shame over her mother's instability, partly because she wants desperately to be a part of the Baum family, and partly because of her feeling of having been abandoned by her real father. No sexual relationship actually did develop with her stepfather or with her stepbrother-as-substitute. The attraction was "successfully" transformed into something else. Yet it is clear that the cost of this adaptation was very high.

In her adult life, when other women would be starting a career and/ or a family, Gail is still like a little child looking in through a window at a family she still wants to be a part of. To an extent that is impossible, particularly now that Robert has remarried and has a daughter by his new wife. Gail is so deeply involved in this unwinnable struggle that for her, maintaining sisterhood is more important than sex.

The Baums are only one stepfamily and a very complex one at that. To discuss some of the issues raised by their story, we must step back a bit and look at the general problem of sexuality in the stepfamily.

### Sexuality in Stepfamilies

Sexuality in stepfamilies is an age-old concern. We find rules regarding it in the Bible. One commandment forbids sexual intercourse with a stepparent: "You shall not uncover the nakedness of your father's wife; it is your nakedness" (Leviticus, 18:8). Soon after comes the rule regarding stepchildren and step-grandchildren; "You shall not uncover the nakedness of a woman and her daughter, and you shall not take her son's daughter or her daughter's daughter to uncover her nakedness; they are your near kinswomen; it is wickedness" (Leviticus, 18:17). The same series of injunctions includes half-siblings: "You shall not uncover the nakedness of your father's wife's daughter, begotten by your father, since she is your sister" (Leviticus, 18:11). One significant thing about Biblical laws, however, is that they do not rule out sexual relations between stepbrothers and stepsisters. Even our ancestors were uncertain about the rules pertaining to stepsibling sexual relations: are they incestuous or not?

As described in the first chapter, step-relations are more ambiguous than those in nuclear families; this ambiguity can be dangerous when it comes to sexuality. Maintaining sexual boundaries is crucial to all families, and drawing them a central task in stepfamilies.

In studying the problem of erotic relations between opposite-sex stepsiblings, the first puzzle is to define what we mean by incest, because different cultures have very different ideas of what constitutes incest. What is more, it is not clear why incest is so universally condemned. Even the tentative answers to these questions are thrown into doubt when we come to stepfamilies in general and stepsiblings in particular. What may define and explain incest in intact nuclear families is much less useful when we are considering the complex world of strangers in the house. Yet stepfamilies do adapt, and the study of how and why they do so reveals some important lessons.

One rule is common to all human societies, the one that prohibits sex between family members. The penalties for violation of the incest taboo are severe. In spite of the immense variation in social life throughout the ages, it seems that we are able to agree on at least one thing—that incest is wrong. But stepfamilies challenge our assumptions about incest and question what the rules regarding sex in remarried families have to be. If the stepfamily is to survive as a viable institution, these rules seem to be most fundamental, and we must try to clarify and understand them.

### What is Incest and Why is it Forbidden?

The commonsense understanding of incest as sexual relations between family members related by blood is adequate only at first sight. Things are not so simple. The close biological relations between parents and children, and between children, are fairly clear. But what about first cousins? What about second cousins and people more distantly related by blood? The line that forbids incestuous relations seems to be drawn rather arbitrarily. We can understand sex being outlawed between brothers and sisters, but permitted between second or third cousins. How about the middle ground—is sex between first cousins incestuous or not? Some cultures, such as our own, regard marriage between first cousins as usually permissible in law but discouraged in practice.[1] Others forbid such marriages. In fact, some primitive societies cast the net of such prohibitions so broadly as to forbid unions that we would regard as entirely acceptable.

The definition of blood relations may vary from one society to the next, but it is not arbitrary. Anthropologists see a link between the importance of family structure to the society and how far the incest taboo spreads outside the parent-child family; for primitive peoples, the extended family is the focus of all economic, political and religious activity. As societies become more advanced, institutions grow up that take the place of the family. In advanced industrial societies such as our own, the responsibilities of the family are reduced to being mere vestiges of what they used to be. The family is less important now than it ever has been before in human history. This may be why the boundaries within which we consider sexual relations to be incestuous are fairly narrow.[2]

Today's family is far weaker than families in the past, yet our society still prohibits sexual relations between blood relatives within it. We share this with all other cultures. Why is the incest taboo still universal?

The simplest explanation is that incest is prohibited for biological reasons, to avoid the deterioration of the species. A child born of a union between parent and child has a higher probability of being born defective, and if this practice continues over more than one generation, the species will very rapidly vanish.[3] But the genetic evidence is that such children could just as likely be born geniuses as idiots. Besides, people have been forbidding incest for far longer than they understood the mechanisms of genetics. The rules prohibiting incest did not follow a period of experimentation, during which the children from incestuous marriages were compared with other children! The rules came first. Another explanation suggests that incest was prohibited because of familiarity, and familiarity, as the common saying goes, breeds contempt.[4] Yet why should the familiarity of spending a long time in the same family lead to "contempt" between siblings but not between the husband and wife themselves? And the incest taboo also pertains to brothers and sisters who may be reared in separate households. Though not reared together, they are still subject to the prohibition.[5]

Freud, in his famous theory of infantile sexuality, takes an entirely different approach.[6] The key to this idea was that all young children have a desire to possess the parent of the opposite sex. This is the celebrated *Oedipus complex* for boys, the *Electra complex* for girls, named for the Greek myths about parent-child incest. The desire is there, but there is no way that it can be consummated. The way out of this dilemma, in its simplest terms, is for a child to suppress these unacceptable thoughts, to "forget" them, although Freud's theory holds that we never forget anything, merely prevent some things from surfacing into our conscious minds. Because the desire is still there, it persists in its influence throughout later life by leading a child to imitate the parent of the same sex, since this person is the victor in the mother-father-child love triangle. This imitation not only leads boys to be masculine like their fathers and girls to be feminine like their mothers, but often in adulthood for them to seek out mates who are in significant ways similar to the opposite sex parent who was coveted but never possessed.

This perspective on incest holds that it stems from desires that all people have in early childhood, but that its fulfillment must be forbidden for children successfully to grow into mature adults by modelling themselves on their like-sex parents. In short, Freud argued that the incest taboo was universal because incestuous desire was universal, and its prohibition indispensible to producing psychologically healthy adults.

This explanation of the incest taboo has recently been questioned by some critics.[7] Whether one accepts Freud's theory in its entirety is not relevant to the sociological question of why the incest taboo is universal. Even if one does accept Freud, this theory does not say anything at all about incest between family members other than parents and children. It says nothing about the prohibition of brother-sister incest, first-cousin sexual relations, stepparent-stepchild incest, or stepsibling incest. It makes a mostly convincing case for explaining why the prohibition of parent-child sexuality is apparently universal, but it does not explain other rules against incest at all.

For an explanation of brother-sister incest prohibitions, we turn, at last, to sociology. Talcott Parsons builds on Freud, reminding us that after the Oedipal conflict has been solved, there follows a period of childhood called "latency," in which all sexual desires are more or less absent and unconscious. The most "symmetrical" arrangement in the family is that at this stage, parents have a "monopoly of erotic relations," and that this more or less total (though temporary) asexuality has to include siblings. In any case, the original object of attraction was the parent of the opposite sex, and once this attraction is repressed, erotic ideas in general disappear.[8]

The latency period is also a time when children increasingly explore social relations outside the family. A lot of this takes place in groups composed of members of the same sex: boys play with boys and girls with girls, and there is frequently considerable disdain shown for one sex by the other. This rigid segregation by sex is a logical outcome of the suppressed erotic attachment to the opposite sex parent and an attempt to emulate the same sex parent. If children in this stage of their lives so compulsively avoid the opposite sex in their play groups, they are going to tend to have an aversion for opposite sex siblings inside the family.

In general terms the incest taboo among pre-teenagers encourages a child to direct his sociability outward and to become confident in associating with people outside the family. Obviously, if he or she is engrossed in a relationship with an opposite-sex peer inside the family, the child will be less likely to achieve competence in social life outside the family. Psychoanalysis explains that the taboo against incest between parent and child is necessary for a person to be psychically and sexually healthy. Sociology explains that the taboo against incest with brothers and sisters, at least before adolescence, is necessary to encourage children to grow socially.

This explanation does not directly justify why erotic relations between teenage brothers and sisters are not allowed, nor, for that matter, why siblings cannot marry when they are adults. In most families, this may simply result from the suppression of conscious sexuality that usually precedes adolescence. The taboo against teenage and adult sibling incest ought simply to be the consequence of the other incest taboos. But some societies in the past, such as the ancient Egyptians, have approved brother-sister marriage, and so we cannot conclude that this taboo is quite as universal as that against parent-child incest.[9] While sexual contact *between* the generations in a family is universally outlawed, sex *within* generations in a family may be viewed somewhat more tolerantly.

Another way to address this question is by looking at the clinical evidence, the conclusions reached by people who treat patients involved in incest who come for help for that or other reasons. Blair and Rita Justice observe that incest between brothers and sisters occurs the most frequently.[10] At the same time, therapists seem to agree that it is probably less harmful, in the long run. Father-daughter incest and mother-son incest are less common, but are far more damaging to the psychological health of the children involved. Brother-sister incest can be damaging, of course, when one of the partners is very young and there is an element of victimization or cruelty involved. But this is true of all pre-teen sex play, whether inside a family or outside it.

Apparently, brother-sister incest is not only not as universally tabooed as parent-child incest, but many therapists do not think of it as being as harmful as incest that crosses generations. The long-term effects of sibling incest may not be as damaging because the social prohibition of them is not as rigid. There is a psychological counterpart to this hypothesis: parent-child incest is damaging because a child depends so utterly on a parent; by comparison, sex play between siblings is less likely to be damaging because siblings are less dependent on one another. If the social taboo against sibling incest is weaker, then the guilt and shame over its violation will be commensurately less. Therapists may sense less social disapproval of this behavior, which is corroborated by the clinical evidence of less damage to children who have been involved in it. Generally speaking, the social prohibition against sibling incest is not as strong as the prohibition of parent-child incest. This is of great importance when we consider the incest taboo as it appears in the stepfamily.

### The Incest Taboo in the Stepfamily

Like the Old Testament, ancient Greek mythology shows a similar concern about stepfamily sex, centered on the erotic attraction between a stepmother and her stepson, in the myth of Phaedra. There are several varieties of this myth, but one of the best known is found in *Hippolytus* by Euripides. Phaedra, a young woman from Crete, marries an older man, King Theseus of Athens, who had previously been married and had a son, Hippolytus. The son had grown up elsewhere, but returned to Athens as a handsome young man, and Phaedra feels strong attraction for him. She does her best to conceal this illicit lust, but a faithful servant tells Hippolytus. He reacts with disgust and curses Phaedra, who commits suicide in despair. She leaves behind a note that falsely accuses Hippolytus of having slept with her. When Theseus reads the letter, he banishes his son, who soon dies in a tragic accident. Theseus subsequently learns that his dead son was really innocent. Later, he, too, meets a violent end.[11]

The concern over sexual attraction between a stepparent and a younger stepchild repeatedly appears in Western literature, too. In the eighteenth century the French playwright Racine took up the Phaedra theme and made it into perhaps his greatest play. In the twentieth century, the American playwright Eugene O'Neill created a similar situation in *Desire Under the Elms*. Vladimir Nabokov's novel *Lolita* shocked many because it portrayed sexual contact with children, but it must be remembered that the crazed Humbert Humbert was Lolita's stepfather.

There are certainly other examples of literary interest in incest in stepfamilies but these are among the best known. They are enough to show that in Western culture, the possibility of sexual attraction between stepfamily members has been in people's consciousness for thousands of years. There are several reasons for this, some of them obvious and some less so.

First, the entire atmosphere of the stepfamily is sexualized. In biological familes, a couple will have passed through the honeymoon period before the children are born. By the time the children are old enough to be consciously aware of sexuality—in their immediately preteen and adolescent years—a couple's ardor will probably have cooled, not necessarily to the point of indifference but almost certainly to the point where they are not visibly infatuated with one another's bodies. In a stepfamily, however, a couple usually goes through its honeymoon in the presence of children. The couple may be discreet enough to avoid any direct display of sexuality, but when a man and a woman are physically fascinated with one another, it is obvious to all, particularly to the watchful eyes of children in the intimate conditions of a household. Adult sexuality, which is usually not an open issue in nuclear families, is right there for all to be aware of in the stepfamily.

What is more, in the stepfamily the stepmother will tend to be closer in age to her stepchildren than their father. We disapprove of women marrying men younger than they, whereas we may approve of a man marrying a younger woman. The increased emphasis of women on careers compounds these effects. Often a career-oriented woman will spend her twenties earning graduate or professional degrees, getting established in a profession, laying the groundwork for achievement. Because most men do not delay marriage to get ahead with their careers, frequently the only marriageable men available to women who have delayed marriage to prepare careers are men who are relatively older, have had children, and gotten divorced. Therefore, when a man remarries, he will tend to marry a woman who is considerably younger than was his first wife. When a remarried man's sons grow into puberty, there is thus a possibility that they will have as a stepmother a woman who is considerably younger than their father and not related by blood to them.

If the taboo against incest means anything, it means a prohibition against sexual activity inside a family. When everyone except the parents inside the family is related by blood, it is a relatively simple proposition to decide who is taboo and who is not. But, as we saw at the beginning of the book, the boundaries of the stepfamily are blurred. It is frequently difficult to decide where the family begins and ends. This is confusing enough in general, but it becomes a serious issue when considering the problems of incest taboos. For instance, if a child's divorced and absent father remarries, are his new wife's children potential mates, or off limits? Are they less available if he moves in with them than if he visits them occasionally? Often the parents themselves cannot decide, and this becomes doubly confusing. One thing is certain, though: if the attraction is there and the rules against it are unclear, there will be a far greater likelihood of people acting on such impulses. The lack of clear family boundaries in the stepfamily is inevitably tied to the incidence of stepfamily incest.

## Stepfamily Sex and the Law[12]

The rules about sex are not clear for the people involved, and they are not clear to the people who make the rules. Although the law has been evolving, the problem is still considered primarily as a question of prohibiting sexual relations between people of unacceptable degrees of *consanguinity*, (blood-relations). What is not always clear and consistent is just what constitutes consanguinity. This relationship can be "lineal" or "collateral." The first is fairly straightforward, and involves direct descent—child, grandchild, and so on. The second involves indirect blood relations, such as aunt and uncle, or nephew and cousin.

Because there is clear lineal descent, the law in America is unanimous in banning parent-child sexual relations. Lineal descent includes siblings as well as parents and children. Half-siblings, too, are considered related in this way. On collateral relations, the law is less consistent. Relations between aunt and nephew and between uncle and niece are specifically prohibited in most state laws. But relations between first cousins are only considered incestuous in some states. In short, outside a commonly agreed-upon core of direct blood relations, U.S. laws prohibiting sexual relations are not always clear and consistent.

When we go beyond lineal and collateral descent to the world of step-relations the law is even more confused. Historically, relations between a stepparent and a stepchild were not regarded as constituting incest. For instance, *in re Bourne*, a 1942 decision in Michigan, held that a father who had sired seven children by four of his stepdaughters was not guilty of incest. More recently, however, laws regarding such matters concentrate less upon degrees of blood relation and more on whether the child in question is in a position to be victimized. A 1983 case, *State of Washington v. Wade Farrington*, decided that stepchildren were descendants and sexual relations between them and a stepparent were forbidden. *Camp v. State of Arkansas*, in 1986, said that "stepchildren and adopted children have been added to the crime of incest because society is concerned with the integrity of the family."

The prohibitions against stepparent-stepchild sex only apply as long as the stepparent is married to the child's parent, because affinity exists only as long as the marriage exists. If the two should divorce, the former stepparent is legally free to marry his or her former stepchild. The only exception to this is that if a woman's stepfather and mother have had a mutual child, she may not marry him after her mother's death, since the birth of a half-sibling establishes an indissoluble consanguineal bond between her and her stepfather. Even when the parent and stepparent are still married, it is not always regarded as incest if the stepson or stepdaughter is of age. In those states where the criterion for incest is blood relation alone, when a stepchild is over the age of twenty-one there is no prohibition of sexual relations with a stepparent (except, of course, that it is considered adultery).

If one considers the new spouse of a noncustodial parent, the situation is even murkier. It is not clear if the new spouse of a noncustodial parent is legally in a parental role, particularly if there is no formal visitation agreement. The actual likelihood of such a relationship developing is quite small—how can a teenage girl, for instance, become infatuated with her absent mother's new husband (or vice-versa) if she does not regularly visit? The point is that the law has no specific prohibition of sexual relations in this case, except as regards the general prohibition of sexual abuse of children and statutory rape. In practical terms, it so happens that women are almost never prosecuted for statutory rape, with the result that the legal sanction against any intercourse between a hypothetical teenage stepson and his noncustodial stepmother would be all but nonexistent.

Thus, in the eyes of the law, being a parent is a permanent status as far as incest is concerned, but being a stepparent must be considered a temporary one, and sexual relations not considered incestuous as such. When it comes to parent-child incest, the legal boundaries of the stepfamily are far more permeable than those of an intact family.

How widespread is parent-child incest, as opposed to stepparent-stepchild incest? In one of the best known studies of the subject, the issue is clouded by the lack of differentiation between father-daughter sexual relations and those between stepfather and stepdaughter. Herman studies the percentage of women who report that that they have been sexually abused by a father *or stepfather*, and the studies she cites give figures ranging from 0 to 1.3 percent. This leads her to assert that one woman in a hundred has suffered from abuse from a father or a stepfather, and she concludes that the incidence of father-daughter incest is therefore alarmingly high. But nowhere does she give a concrete estimate of the number of females who have encountered real father-daughter incest. Since we know that the prohibition against stepfather-stepdaughter incest is weaker than real father-daughter incest, we must infer that the former probably accounts for most of the reported incidents. Real father-daughter incest is therefore probably extremely rare, which we should expect, given the strong legal and social objections to it.[13]

Other data corroborate this inference. One report avers that there is some evidence that abuse (both sexual and nonsexual) is more likely in stepfamilies, and that stepfathers are more likely to be the perpetrators than fathers. But so are mothers; the 1981 National Incidence Study of Child Abuse and Neglect cited in this report says that mothers were involved in 43 percent of the cases of sexual abuse, compared to 28 percent of the incidents involving fathers.[14]

Diana Russell's highly selective study inquires into sexual contact between females and any male relative. In this survey, 778 women in San Francisco were willing to respond out of a total of 930 contacted; 181 reported some form of sexual contact with a male relative. The author concludes that of the women who said that they were raised by a stepfather with whom they lived, 17 percent (out of a total number of 29) had sexual contact with a stepfather, but that of the women who mentioned a biological father as "primary caretaker" "only 2.3 percent were sexually abused by him before the age of fourteen." Taking into account that Russell found that only a small proportion of the "sexual abuse" cases involved sexual intercourse, it is quite clear that actual father-daughter coition is extremely rare. Stepfather-stepdaughter sexual contact, it was found, was relatively more common, and was more likely to consist of more than a single incident. In light of the unclear taboos involved for all participants in stepfamilies, this is not surprising.[15]

Sex between siblings and half-siblings is forbidden, but there are no states where sexual relations between stepsiblings constitute incest. The only exception is where one of the parties is not of legal age of consent. In themselves, the relations of affinity between stepsiblings are such that there are no grounds for prohibiting sex between them. This is so even when the stepsiblings have been adopted by their stepparents. A 1978 decision in Colorado, *Martin and Tammy Israel v. Allen*, for instance, dealt with whether or not a stepbrother and stepsister could marry each other after their adoptive stepparents had died. The decision said, in part, "The objections that exist against consanguineous marriages are not present where the relationship is merely by affinity. The physical detriment to the offspring of persons related by blood is totally absent. . . ." It is apparent that, for the law, there is no such thing as incest between stepsiblings in the United States.[16]

## Stepsibling Sex: Uncertainty Among Therapists

While families are confused about stepsibling sex, and the law is relatively uncertain, family therapists are not certain, either. One of the pilot studies carried out in preparation of this book was a mailed survey of marital and family therapists, in which a question was asked about stepsibling incest. While some of the twenty-seven respondents agreed that erotic attraction between stepsiblings was a problem in stepfamilies, three specifically wrote on the questionnaire that such a relationship is not incestuous, because there is no blood tie. In one of the most widely used handbooks written to help therapists with stepfamilies, the authors state, "Sexual experiences between stepsiblings need to be evaluated but are not necessarily cause for alarm."[17] Esther Wald, while not discounting the disruptive effects of intra-stepfamily sex, argues that a differentiation needs to be made between "real" incest between blood relations and "technical" incest between step-relatives.[18] It seems that even among professionals, whom we might expect to have a clearer idea of what is and is not permitted in stepfamilies, there is less than unanimous agreement and no categorical certainty.

The psychological viewpoint of Freud gives another reason why the rules of incest are less clear in the stepfamily. If the Oedipus and Electra complexes are resolved the way they are supposed to be, a child banishes from conscious thought his attraction to his parent of the opposite sex. This mental process is at work for the rest of a person's family and life history. It is the backdrop, as it were, of all the family dramas that follow. In the case of the stepfamily, of course, such an Oedipal history is absent. In the biological family it takes place when a child is at a particular stage in his psychic development. There is a sequence of events in the formation of one's personality, and early childhood is the appropriate stage. For such erotic attraction to be successfully suppressed when one is later in childhood or in adolescence is quite unlikely.

The sibling incest taboo, presumably, follows from the general suppression of erotic feelings during later childhood and the fact that sibling incest is prohibited as part of the general prohibition of sexuality within the family. But we saw that the taboo against incest between siblings is not as universal and as strong as that against parent-child incest. If there is a lack of common Oedipal history between a stepchild and his stepparent, there is also a lack of common Oedipal history with stepsiblings. The psychological backdrop to the stepfamily drama is not the same. We should therefore expect that, in addition to the weaker social and legal taboos, there is less psychological resistance to stepsibling incest than to sibling incest.

Thus, incest is always a central issue in families, and its prohibition is socially and psychologically necessary. Stepfamilies, however, encounter the problem of unclear rules about what is permitted and not permitted, not only from an ambiguous legal system, but (insofar as they ever consult them at all) from therapists who are dealing with families in such a state of instability and uncertainty. For stepsiblings, the confusion is even greater. Such confusion is not simply an intellectual problem; it is a dilemma that has to be overcome if the newly-formed family is to survive.

### The Stepfamily's Sexual Dilemma

We can now see that, regarding sex in the family, our society perceives several degrees of incest, some of which are regarded as more serious and others less so. The "most incestuous" type of sexual relationship is that between biological parent and child, which is regarded as psychologically most damaging by professionals and which is also clearly forbidden by law. Next comes brother-sister sex, which is legally prohibited, but is relatively more common than parent-child incest, and is regarded as somewhat less damaging. Following that comes stepparent-stepchild incest, which is forbidden on the grounds that sexual contact between adults and children is undesirable, whether they are in the same legally constituted family or not. Last comes stepsibling sex. Not only is it not against the law; some do not regard it as incestuous. The Bible has no prohibition against it and neither does the Jewish Talmud, the commentary on the first five books of the Old Testament. The legal barriers are nonexistent, the social disapproval less intense, and even the psychic resistance to it is relatively weak, in comparison to the other types.

How can a family function, though, if the parents do not maintain the "monopoly of erotic relations" that seems to be so important? How can the children in a family be induced to direct their erotic attachments outwards, and to develop their social skills outside the family, when there is the active possibility of an intense attachment forming between siblings unrelated by blood? A family cannot carry out one of its basic jobs, developing psychologically healthy and socially adapted children, unless it outlaws sex between stepsiblings. This, then, is the fundamental dilemma of the stepfamily: *A stepfamily must manufacture its own stepsibling incest taboo in the absence of a societal stepsibling incest taboo.*

Resolving this dilemma is a specific example of what stepfamilies must do in general, which is to make up their own rules for survival in the absence of rules provided by the society around it. Usually, there is a "fit" between the rules that generally apply in a society and the rules that operate within a family. In the case of the stepfamily, the situation is quite different. With no clear guidelines, each stepfamily must try to work out norms of behavior, isolated from other families around it. It is not surprising that some stepfamilies fail at this. What is encouraging is that most succeed.

This discussion only concerns heterosexual relations between stepsiblings. Homosexual relations, while stringently tabooed, are not impossible. One respondent to the SAA survey said, "My oldest (and only) stepson is gay and I can tell you I was damn nervous about leaving him alone (which I *rarely* did) with my other sons." Of course, heterosexual relations are the main potential source of tensions.

At least three possible patterns appear in response to the sexualized atmosphere of the stepfamily and the relative absence of the stepsibling incest taboo. The first is that stepsiblings may engage in sexual activity. Or, second, their sexual feelings may be so frightening that they surface in the form of pretended indifference or hostility. The third possiblity is that they may successfully transform their erotic emotions into a warm, nonsexual relationship.[19] Let us examine each of these.

### Sexual Relations Between Stepsiblings

Stepsiblings sometimes do actually enter into some sort of sexual relationship, one that may be temporary or may develop into something more serious. It is hard to tell how widespread this is.

There has been no systematic sociological study of stepsibling incest, although the study of Diana Russell referred to above does provide some indirect information. She reports that of the female "victims" of sexual contact with a male relative, twenty-five had had this experience with a brother. Of these twenty-five cases, one was with a stepbrother and one was with a half-brother. Neither of the cases involved sexual intercourse, and both consisted of a single incident. Her figures suggest that roughly 3 percent of women in stepfamilies have had some sort of stepsibling sex and roughly the same percent half-sibling sex.[20]

However, Russell's sample is much too biased for us to infer much from it about the real incidence of stepsibling and half-sibling sexual relations in stepfamilies in general. Her sample was restricted to San Francisco, it was comprised of a sample of women (out of a considerably larger sample) who were willing to talk about previous sexual experiences with total strangers, it always construed a female participant in sexual activity as a "victim," it claimed any type of remotely sexual contact as "abuse," and it was deliberately slanted to evoke negative feelings from respondents. We cannot say with any certainty if the sample is representative; at the same time, the purpose of the survey, the wording of the questions, and the interpretation of the responses were obviously polemical. Also, it surveyed adult women, who were children and adolescents at a time when stepfamilies were far less prevalent than they are now. Simply on that basis alone, we should suspect that there is more stepsibling sexual behavior than Russell uncovered. Her survey does not really provide a clear answer to the question of the incidence or effects of stepsibling sexuality. Lacking this sort of information for a whole population, we must look at the subject from the point of view of people who treat stepfamilies in which sexual tension becomes problematic.

For more insight into the origins and implications of stepsibling incest, we turn to clinical evidence. Sexuality is one of the major issues for children in remarried families, particularly children in late childhood and adolescence. Part of the problem is that even when sex is a disturbing issue, the adults in a stepfamily do not want to face it, not only because they may be uncomfortable with their own sexuality but also because they regard it as something that should not arise in a "normal" family. As we saw at the beginning of the book, one of the main sources of problems in stepfamilies is the insistence by adults that it is a family like all others. This is particularly inappropriate in the area of intrafamilial sexuality, where the stepfamily is very difficult from the nuclear family. Here is one area where it is especially clear that pretending the stepfamily is no different from the nuclear family will result in pretending to ignore feelings that are urgent and disruptive.

For teenage stepsiblings, as for all teenagers, sexual feelings are often disturbing. The common alienation that teenagers feel from their stepfamilies may be rooted in an attempt to avoid incestuous impulses. Very often, the feelings of rebelliousness against the stepfamily will intensify with the onset of a stepteen's sexual maturity. A mystified stepparent will say "We got along fine" until something happened. For a stepdaughter that "something" will often be the onset of menstruation. Sexual maturity will produce unwelcome feelings about stepsiblings as well as stepparents.[21]

Lacking a clear moral message, what is "wrong" with stepsibling incest? Teenagers in general find real sexual activity overwhelming, particularly in early adolescence. They have particular difficulty distinguishing between a purely sexual relationship and a nurturant one arising between two separate and mature people. Sociological studies confirm this psychological axiom, showing that women who began sexual activity before the age of sixteen have significantly higher rates of sexual and psychological dissatisfaction, and more marital discord and divorce than normal.[22] Youngsters may be physically equipped for sex, but premature sex often has lasting detrimental effects.

Sibling or stepsibling incest interferes with the process through which people go out into the world in search of a suitable partner. An *enmeshment* takes place. The relationship inside the family is so intense that an adolescent is not released from his family. Enmeshment therefore prevents a family from accomplishing one of its basic functions, to equip young people for departure into a social world in which they can act as independent individuals.

These observations could be used to argue against sexual involvement of siblings as well as stepsiblings, and they illustrate how both must be forbidden for a family to function. In the particular case of stepsibling incest it can provide a way for stepchildren to carry out warfare with a stepparent through indirect means. If a boy has been "the man of the family" for a long time, he will resent the intrusion of his stepfather into his territory. The psychic consequence of his rivalry is to covet something that belongs to his stepfather, such as his stepfather's daugher. In such a situation, the daughter herself is not really an object of affection or attraction at all, but is simply a weapon on the battlefield between stepchild and stepparent. The Baums provide an example of the obverse, where a stepsibling can be a substitute for a coveted stepparent.

Finally, sexual activity between adolescent stepsiblings cannot fail to be perceived by other siblings. In the case of younger siblings or stepsiblings, this results in an inappropriate and precocious stimulation of their own sexuality. Sexual feelings are provoked in pre-teens before they emerge naturally, which in turn can produce promiscuity and other signs of sexual maladjustment. In summary, abundant psychological and sociological grounds exist for concluding that stepsibling sexual activity cannot be permitted, even though society at large is not vigorous in its condemnation.

What happens when stepsiblings actually do have sexual relations? Brenda Maddox describes one stepfamily in which the parents stoutly denied that the relation was incestuous, and another where, in spite of strong feelings of outrage on the part of other stepsiblings, they simply pretended that it was not happening. These relations were not just disruptive on the parent-stepparent-stepchild plane, but between and among siblings and stepsiblings as well.[23]

In other cases, though, it develops farther, with serious consequences. An interviewed New York social worker cites a case involving sexual intercourse between stepsiblings. A divorced and remarried woman, Joy, had a nineteen-year-old son, Charles, as well as a young adult daughter and a mutual child, living in her home. Joy also had a sixteen-year-old stepdaughter, Maureen, living in the home. Charles and Maureen became very close, at first because he was very comforting to the girl, whose mother had died. Eventually, they started sleeping together, and Charles began acting as the girl's guardian within the family. "The two of them are now so powerful that Joy and her husband can't do anything. He's kind of in charge of her, he decides if she goes out. . . He's jealous when she goes out. But he's in charge of it, not the parents," says the therapist. At present, Charles and Maureen are such a strong team that Joy and her husband have no authority over either of them in the household.[24]

Although this is only a single case, it illustrates the consequences when the incest taboo is not maintained between stepsiblings. In this case, the formation of another eroticized couple in addition to the remarried parents unquestionably undermined the cohesion of the household. The influence of stepparents in a remarried family is usually quite limited anyway, since often obedience and authority follow blood ties. In addition, the adult couple often have difficulty functioning as a unit. This already attenuated power may be reduced to virtually nothing if there is another quasi-adult team set up by emotionally and physically involved stepteens. Such a challenge to adult authority may be too much for the new couple to withstand, which is all the more reason why stepsibling sex must be outlawed if the stepfamily is to have any kind of stability at all.

In fact, youngsters in stepfamilies do not usually act on their urges. Rather, a second outcome is much more likely, that the teenage stepsiblings will convert their troubling erotic urges into hostility. Conscious animosity toward the object of their desire becomes a means of protecting themselves from their feelings.

### Stepsibling Hostility: A Way of Coping

Parents are frequently mystified by the degree of antagonism between their adolescent children and stepchildren. In one of the stepfamily self-help groups that was observed in research for this book, the most frequent phrase quoted to describe stepteen feelings was, "They hate each other." Almost as frequent was a carefully studied avoidance. As one stepteen said succinctly, "You keep it simple. . . like, 'Pass the salt.' " Another stepmother, after remarking on the seething stepsibling hostility in her household, also observed, almost offhandedly, "My daughter never walked around the house after a shower with only a towel on before Paul [her stepbrother] came!" Erotic attraction may in fact be the root of much stepsibling hostility.

Hostility inside the family is not the only place where such displaced sexuality is manifested. School behavior with peers and attitudes towards authority are also areas where this anger can be manifested. Drugs, promiscuity, poor academic performance, getting in trouble with the police—all are avenues through which expression of unacceptable stepsibling attraction can be shown.

Anger is an almost inevitable part of adolescence. It is part of the process whereby a teenager gradually distances himself from his family.[25] "Normal" teenage anger can serve a purpose in helping a child to sever the ties that bound him to his parents and to establish himself as an autonomous person. Anger that results from intense feelings of stepsibling attachment does not represent a severing of the person from the family, rather, it is a clear indication of just how closely involved he or she is. Anger that comes from enmeshment does not free a person, but can more closely bind him or her to the family, at exactly the stage in life when breaking free is the most important task.

Anger between stepteens is as difficult to handle as sexual attraction. Never a welcome emotion for anyone, for stepteens anger can be particularly explosive, not only because of its frightening implications but because of the power stepchildren feel they have. Family therapists repeatedly remark about how, for children of divorce, angry exchanges are associated with family breakup. He or she may fear that the expression of anger will threaten the stability of the new family or might even "cause" it to collapse.[26]

Though this may not sound plausible at first, it is not so absurd from the stepteen's point of view. Stepchildren have considerably more power in the family than children in other families—partly because the authority of the stepparent is subordinate to the parent, and partly because children often sense that if it came to a crunch, a biological parent would have a hard time deciding between the child and the new spouse. This, of course, feeds the persistent fantasy of splitting up the remarried couple with an eye to reuniting the biological parents. With this emotional backdrop, it is not so ridiculous that stepchildren in general, and stepteens in particular, imagine that the expression of their anger might make or break the new family. This power is terrifying, not only because adolescents are unprepared for it, but because they often want to establish membership in the newly formed family. Therefore, the anger itself has to be suppressed, and may find its way into sullen indifference, or expression of hostility in the outside world (through drug and alcohol abuse, vandalism or other anti-social activity). Or it can go in an inward direction, and result in a compulsive over-conformity, in which a stepteen feels he must rigidly conform in order to safeguard his place in the family and the stability of the family itself.

The foregoing description of the pattern of adjustment, while complex, is still too simple to describe what actually happens. Stepteens are changing, evolving people, and so are their relationships. The responses from the SAA survey illustrate this variation. For some stepfamilies, the fact that there are opposite sex stepsiblings is merely a technicality, since their age differences are so great. As one stepparent said, "They usually interact very little. There is a four-year age span, which may create such a large gulf at this particular time that the oldest thinks of the younger as a 'kid.'" Still, the story of the Baums reminds us that there is considerable potential for erotic attraction even when one stepsibling is much younger than the other.

One mother wrote that the relationship between her stepchild and natural child "swings from hostility to indifference." Her perception was that, "Since they are nine months apart, most of their fighting seems to be normal sibling rivalry, not much different than teens in original families that I know." And where there are several stepteens involved in the same family, the nature of the relationships can be quite different. One mother answered, "There are two such relationships in our household, each very different. One, which is between a fourteen-year-old boy and his fifteen-year-old stepsister, is characterized by mutual respect. They seem to genuinely like each other and will do nice things for each other if the opportunity presents itself. The other relationship, however, is quite different. This is between a seventeen-year-old boy and the same girl. The girl is openly hostile toward the boy, with sarcastic remarks. The boy reacts indifferently towards the girl unless pushed very far, then a nasty verbal exchange will take place."

Several responses indicate that neither the dangerous alternative of sexual relations nor the disruptive behavior of hostility emerge. "Indifference" was by far, the adjective most frequently circled by respondents asked to describe the behavior of opposite-sex stepteens toward each other. In the case of one relationship between stepsiblings that was characterized this way, the respondent indicated that there was "no sexual attraction between the children" and that "there are no major conflicts between my thirteen-year-old son and his eleven-year-old stepsister." Another described the relations as "friendly, compatible, indifferent." A third said that the relationship was one of affection and that the boy and girl were "very close." The respondent father went on, "Both are very close, same age and in the same grade in high school. They talk to each other about whatever." One of the descriptions was so rational as to be slightly suspect. The relationship was stated to be one of "cooperative mutuality," and in response to the question about how the issue of sexual attraction had been resolved or coped with, the stepparent wrote, "They talked it out and resolved that they prefer to maintain a sibling relationship." One suspects that it was not really as smooth as that, and that the adult may not have perceived all that was going on.

These adaptations seem comparatively successful, but if sexuality is always a latent issue in situations such as this, it must have been disposed of somehow. The indifference is probably not as sincere as appears at first sight. And the affection may be a sublimated form of attraction, a transformation of sex into sentiment.

### Redirected Sex: A Successful Adaptation?

Tom Sterling is an eighteen-year-old college student. His father passed away when he was twelve years old. He and his older brother Dennis, subsequently lived alone with his mother, Jesse. Jesse had joined a group called Parents Without Partners, where she met Sean, a widower with two daughters, Diana, who is five months older than Tom, and Dierdre, who is ten years older. When Tom was fourteen and Dennis was eighteen, Jesse and Sean married. By that time Dierdre had married and had a child. Dennis went away to college about a year after the marriage. For the past four years, then, Tom has lived in a household consisting of his mother, his stepfather and his stepsister Diana. He rarely sees Dierdre, his other stepsister, who is estranged from his stepfather.

At the beginning, Diana resented Tom's mother. "Me and my brother used to look in her diary. I mean I really shouldn't have done this, but. . . We used to go in her room, my brother and me, and I remember reading a couple of pages, 'I hate Jesse, she's stealing my Dad, and so on. . .'" But they get along well now. "These feelings have pretty much evaporated. They get along great now." Tom himself was fond of his stepfather from the start. "I liked the guy as soon as I met him. My mother had gone out with some nice guys and I liked him immediately, because having two daughters he knew kids and he knew how to react." Dennis had reservations about Sean. "I should say that he didn't like the idea too much that they were getting married. He had written down some letters that he never sent, and he wrote about how he felt as if he were looking at a stranger. He still feels deep inside, 'You're not my father,' but gets along with them."

The most important relationship for our discussion here is Tom's interaction with Diana. "We seem to have gotten along from the beginning. I remember when we first moved into the apartment, I kind of thought of her as like a bitch. Because she did act like a bitch, you know. She can be very moody, and I'm not very moody. I'm generally in a good mood. I guess we would kind of rub each other the wrong way. But that was a couple of years ago, and pretty much we have gotten along. I should say that we have really gotten very close. A lot of times, you know, it's good to have a girl your age in the house because a lot of times I needed advice on girls—now what do I do, now where do I take her tonight—I don't know what to do. She was there and we were both more than happy to help each other out.

In response to the question, "Did you ever feel attracted to her?" Tom indicated that he had given some thought to the problem. "Incest and stuff like that. In the beginning I didn't think that much of her. But she is cute, you know, although I think she ought to do more for her personal appearance. I felt that she was cute. . . . If she wasn't my stepsister. . . But I just kept thinking that."

*Author:* How about Diana? Do you think she was attracted to you?

*Tom:* I thought she was, at times. But maybe that was just in my head.

*Author:* You never came out and talked about it?

*Tom:* No, because it was just like if you pass somebody on the street and say 'Hey, that girl is nice, but I can never see her again.' You wouldn't really think about it. That was just in the back of my head, 'Oh, she's cute.'

*Author:* Did Sean ever say anything to you about it?

*Tom:* No, because they never had any reason to.

*Author:* Did your relationship change over time? At first, you mentioned that she seemed rather moody and irritating, but then after awhile things changed.

*Tom:* I guess because she changed as a person. We started high school at the same time, and I guess she changed from an immature teeny bopper and she became mature and I guess she learned how to deal with life. I guess she changed as a person.

For Tom and Diana, obviously, erotic attraction is an issue never far from the surface. Without receiving any explicit directions from their parents, though, they appear to have worked out a *modus vivendi*. Although "a bitch" at first—one wonders how Diana would describe their relations at the beginning—Diana has come to be a valuable person to Tom. She provides vital information about the opposite sex. Not that a blood sister would be unable to provide similar informtion, but there seems to be a safer distance between Tom and Diana so that they can serve as resources for one another in growing through adolescence. They are "very close" and they "are happy to help each other out."

Thus, a third possibility that emerges from the sexual attraction between stepsiblings is a warm, nonerotic tie between them. Duberman says that in her research stepsiblings whose relationship was reported as "excellent" by stepparents was the least frequent. Indifference and hostility were more common; the fact that sets of stepsiblings lived together was apparently important in increasing the likelihood that they would get along well together.[27]

Although there may be attraction at first between adolescent oppo-site-sex stepsiblings who are living together, this is likely to lead to a safer, and even closer, relationship. One SAA respondent said, "There seemed to be a sexual attraction at first between my son (age 15) and stepdaughter (age 13). I feel this is not a concern of ours because they seem to have developed a friendship. I have spoken with my son re-garding his feelings. He has no sexual feelings toward her. Possibly my stepdaughter feels an attraction to my son. They have formed a unique bond. I could best describe it as a friendship. They enjoy the same friends and seem to communicate better than other stepsiblings in the family."

A young woman named Linda, interviewed in the survey of college-age stepsiblings, was remarkable in this regard. Linda's mother and father had divorced when she was in later childhood. Subsequently her father remarried and she regularly visited her father, his new wife, and her three sons by a previous marriage, all of whom were older than she—in their early to mid-adolescence. Linda developed a very close relationship with the three boys, to the extent that she insisted they were her "brothers." She explained that she had learned a lot about growing up from them, and that she often took problems to them for solution, even problems of a fairly intimate nature. She still visits them regularly, even though she is now in her early twenties. Near the end of the inteview, almost as an afterthought, Linda mentioned that her father was now divorced again, had moved to a midwestern city, and married for a third time! In the process of growing through adolescence with stepbrothers, she had successfully channeled her attraction to one or more of them into a very close emotional bond, symbolized by her insistence on calling them brothers, even after there ceased to be any formal relationship between them.

Linda's situation allows us to look at the problem of stepsibling eroticism in the whole context of adolescent development. Sex, anger, and deep attachment are all the signs of an entanglement that can have consequences for a youngster's development. Breaking away from the family in gradual stages is the natural process of being a teenager. It involves successive attempts to pretend that one is an adult, while at the same time needing adults to pay the bills, do the laundry, and put food on the table. A teenager may visit a shopping mall with her family, but insist that they not be seen together by her friends, pretending to others and herself that she is shopping alone. The same person will purchase clothing, makeup, and records with her father's credit card, and not see that as a threat to her adult status. All the while, an adolescent will need to be able to retreat into the childlike role, expecting warmth, affection, and uncritical support from parents.

Adolescence is doubly difficult for children in stepfamilies, because they are burdened by two major conflicting tasks: establishing themselves as independent people while at the same time joining the newly made family. Such a contradiction is not as acute for a teenager who has joined a stepfamily at a relatively early age. But even then, the onset of sexual maturity can provoke the resurfacing of a lot of issues that everyone thought were settled. As a general rule, a stepteen must go in two directions at the same time, both leaving and entering the stepfamily.

The psychic enmeshments of sexual attraction and sexually-inspired hostility interfere with this process. A teenager will have a much more difficult time breaking away from the family if he or she is involved in a sexually-based relationship with a stepsibling, whether this shows itself as flirting and provocative behavior or as hostility and cold avoidance. The stepfamily cannot then be the stable launching platform from which an adolescent takes off into the world, because there are emotional cables that bind him and prevent his free movement.

The long-term effects of this involvement can be seen repeatedly among siblings from stepfamilies. One of the most remarkable traits of stepsiblings is the extent to which, even in their mid- to late twenties, they still consider the network of the stepfamily as the most important set of relationships in their lives. It is not possible to give a precise numerical figure for this, of course, because it refers to something that, at least to date, has not been measured. But therapists and stepsiblings themselves regularly recognize how deeply involved stepsiblings are with their families, how difficult it seems for them to break away.

These observations allow us to make some final comments on the complex relationships among the Baums. Gail and William are clearly infatuated with one another. Gail's attachment to William is a by-product of her love for her stepfather. This, in turn, results from the deeply scarring effects of her mother's stormy relationship with Robert, in which Gail felt her mother was wrong and her stepfather was right. As if to atone for her mother's misbehavior she almost attempted to take her place in her stepfather's affections. Gail's frustrated attachment to her stepfather, transmitted into an acknowledged but unfulfilled longing for her stepbrother, has resulted in a frantic but hopeless struggle to actually cease being a Donovan and become a Baum. With regard to overconformity, it is important to recall her remark that she felt superior to all of her stepsiblings and natural siblings, because she was the one closest to Robert. By being a good little girl, she retains the hope that she will be granted admission to membership in her step-father's family, even though he long ago divorced her mother.

The Baums have been used as an example with which to begin and conclude this chapter because much discussion of intrafamily relations can become too schematic and simplistic. In spite of the fact that we can discern patterns and make generalizations, as summarized below, it must be kept in mind that stepsibling relationships are extraordinarily complex, and that there will always be exceptions to even the most general rules.

### Conclusion: The Incest Taboo and Stepsiblings

Sexual feelings play a large part in the dynamics of any family. From the beginning of our lives, through the latency period, to the reemergence of adult sexuality, they are a basic feature of our emotional development. The stepfamily complicates all of these issues. Step-children, unless they become part of a stepfamily at an extremely early age, interact with stepparents with whom they have not experienced the psychological evolution that provides sexual boundaries in the intact family. Relations with stepsiblings also do not have the same history, the dramas that take place between them do not have the same "scenery."

Human society has always condemned overt sexual relations between kin, although the definition of kin has changed as the family has shrunk in its social importance. The incest taboo today includes only biologically related parent and child, biologically related children and half-brothers and half-sisters. And even sex between siblings is not seen as quite so wrong, quite so damaging as between parent and child. The incest taboo applies still more weakly between members of step-families. The law, a crude indicator of social morals, prohibits sex between stepparent and stepchild (though it usually does not specify that it is incest) and between half-siblings. But it generally does not see sex between stepsiblings as incestuous at all.

At the same time, any family, if it is to be successful in teaching its young to go out into the social world and to give them the motivation to do so, must prohibit sex between anyone but adults. The stepfamily must enforce these ground rules as well. This constitutes a fundamental dilemma of the stepfamily with regard to sex among its members: it must manufacture and maintain its own familial incest taboo in the absence of a strong societal incest taboo.

Thus, in practice, three outcomes are possible to the sexual attraction that inevitably will appear between stepsiblings in their pre-teen or teenage years. The first is that the youngsters will actually initiate sexual relations. This cannot continue, not only because it is so disruptive to everyday family life, but because the partners themselves are likely to be unable to cope with it. As in the case cited above, either the parents or the children themselves will be obliged to separate the stepsiblings involved, requiring one of them to live elsewhere. Of course, this does not necessarily "resolve" the situation, but it makes for more family stability. The attraction between the people involved may continue, but if it does, it may be more acceptable to adults and youngsters alike, because it can be seen as more of a dating relationship between two unrelated people, and consequently more "normal."

More likely is that the teenagers will be so disturbed by their feelings of attraction that the feelings will not even be conscious; rather they will be consciously felt as hostility. Different methods of distancing are used to push away the object of this desire, which can range from sullen avoidance and cold politeness to dislike and rage. The boy who said that it was best to stick to basics, like "Please pass the salt," was demonstrating what can be the safest adaptation. Yet this, too, does not mean that the issue has been resolved, particularly because normal teenage anger can be escalated to the point of being socially dangerous and may impede an adolescent's learning social skills. It is safer to be hostile than to show attraction, but in the long run it can be harmful. At the very least, it makes the stepfamily a scene of confrontation and tension.

Because anger can be such a disturbing sign of family instability, and a reminder of the stepchild's power over adults, the anger itself may be rigidly controlled and replaced by a compulsive over-conformity. Such stepteens may be perceived in the short run as paragons of adolescent adjustment, but the long-term costs can be unbearable. An adolescent stepsibling who does not permit himself or herself any rebelliousness at all is far more maladjusted than one who occasionally jumps over the traces. The effort involved in entirely controlling one's emotions is such that one may not have the energy to do much else in life. At the very least, it results in difficulties in breaking away from the stepfamily.

Finally, children can transform their feelings of attraction into a warm, nonerotic relationship. This is probably the best outcome that can be hoped for. It allows the family to function normally, both in its own eyes and in the eyes of society at large. Siblings can be deeply attached to one another, and provide supportive relationships that last a lifetime. The adolescent stepsibling who has succeeded in expressing his or her sexual attraction in the form of a tie that is deeper than that which often appears between siblings, has reached a compromise that makes the best of a difficult situation.

Yet even here, in the best solution, there are pitfalls. Teenage stepsiblings are trying to do two things at the same time: to join the stepfamily and to break away as independent people. The deep enmeshment that takes place when sexual attraction is turned into deep sibling friendship can be a difficult barrier.

The first part of the book looked at the ways in which sibling rivalry appears between stepsiblings. Of course, this rivalry can become bitter and unresolved, but as we have seen, its outcome can sometimes be the process of "deidentification," when stepsiblings learn who they are by comparing themselves to people they choose to be different from. This is not necessarily a happy result, but it can help children in the difficult task of shaping an identity for themselves. The second part looked at the problem of a child's losing his place in age-order when the stepfamily is formed. If sibling and stepsibling rivalry both stem from competition over the scarce resources of space, property, love, and attention, this part looks at one of the most important ways in which children rank themselves in the family hierarchy: birth order and age order. One way to resolve a prince losing his throne or a policeman losing his beat is for children to maintain birth order even though they have lost place in the age order. The foregoing chapter has looked at the other side of stepsibling rivalry, as it were, the problem of stepsibling sexuality. It, too, shows that there are no easy solutions to the situation, but that some are better than others.

In the next part, we turn to a type of sibling relations in the stepfamily that in some ways is similar, but which also has an additional characteristic. In stepsibling relations there is no blood tie, and this lack is linked to the problems we have discussed. In many stepfamilies, the remarried spouses have a child in common. This means that a half-sibling has been born, but the fact that it is related by blood to the other children does not mean that it is like other sibling relations. The half-sibling has a role that needs to be discussed in its own right.

### Notes

1. Michael Einbinder, "The Legal Family—A Definitional Analysis," *Journal of Family Law* 13 (1973–74):781–802, esp. p. 783 and footnote on p. 782.
2. See Leslie White, "The Definition and Prohibition of Incest," *American Anthropologist* 50 (July–September 1948):416–35.
3. Lewis Morgan, *Ancient Society* (New York: Holt, 1978), pp. 69, 378, 424.
4. Edvard Westermarck, *The History of Human Marriage* (London: Macmillan, 1921), Ch. 20.

5. Brenda Maddox, *The Half-Parent* (New York: Evans, 1975).
6. Ernest Jones, *The Life and Work of Sigmund Freud* (Garden City: Doubleday, 1963), pp. 206–7.
7. Jeffrey Masson, *The Assult on Truth: Freud's Suppression of the Seduction Theory* (New York: Farrar, Straus, & Giroux, 1984).
8. Talcott Parsons, "The Incest Taboo in Relation to Social Structure," in Rose Coser ed., *The Family: Its Structure and Functions* (New York: St. Martin's, 1974), pp. 26–27.
9. Russell Middleton, "A Deviant Case: Brother-Sister and Father-Daughter Marriage in Ancient Egypt," in Coser, *The Family*, p. 31–43.
10. Blair Justice and Rita Justice, *The Broken Taboo* (New York: Human Sciences, 1972), esp. p. 193.
11. Alfred Messer, "The Phaedra Complex," in *Archives of General Psychiatry* 21 (August 1969):213–18.
12. My thanks to Ms. Lana Rottenberg of the Cardozo School of Law, Yeshiva University, for her research assistance in preparing this chapter.
13. Judith Herman, *Father-Daughter Incest* (Cambridge: Harvard University Press, 1981).
14. Jean Giles-Sims and David Finkelhor, "Child Abuse in Stepfamilies," *Family Relations* 33 (July 1984):407–13.
15. Diana Russell, *The Secret Trauma: Incest in the Lives of Girls and Women* (Basic Books, 1986), pp. 233–35.
16. See also Leigh Bienen, "The Incest Statutes," Appendix to Herman, 1981, *Father-Daughter Incest.*
17. Clifford Sager et al., *Treating the Remarried Family* (New York: Brunner and Mazel, 1983) p. 258.
18. Wald, 1981, *Remarried Family*, p. 109.
19. Marilyn Kent, "Remarriage: A Family Systems Perspective," *Social Casework* 61 (March 1980):146–53.
20. Russell, 1986, *Secret Trauma*, pp. 280–81.
21. My thanks to Dr. Craig Brown, a child psychologist in Syosset, Long Island, for explaining these features of stepfamily sexuality.
22. Carol Tavris and Susan Sadd, *The Redbook Report on Female Sexuality* (New York: Delacorte, 1975), pp. 48–49, 58.
23. Maddox, 1975, *Half-Parent*, p. 106–7; and Wald, 1981, *Remarried Family*, p. 108.
24. My thanks to Ms. Margot Weinshel, social worker in New York City, for explaining this case.
25. My thanks to New York social worker Joseph Moore for explaining many of the dimensions of stepteen experience during a workshop he organized at the 1985 Annual Meeting of the Stepfamily Association of America in Chevy Chase, Maryland.
26. Linda Craven, *Stepfamilies*, p. 109.
27. Duberman, *Stepkin-relationships* and *Reconstituted Family*.

# 5

# The Birth of a Half-Sibling: Boon or Bane?

> *When my parents were together there was a lot of fighting. It was really embarrassing for me and my brother. We would run up to our rooms. My father would go on these long business trips. I didn't get to see him a lot. Right after they got divorced, my mom was working a lot. I didn't get to see her much. I saw my father every weekend and whenever I had to go I'd get really scared. I'd start screaming, 'You're taking me away from Mommy!' Now I get to see them both equally. My mom doesn't work because she just had a baby. When she told me she was pregnant, I was jumping all around. I was really excited. I don't call him my half-brother, I call him my real brother. I like it.*
>
> —Lizbeth, age 11

Lizbeth is more the rule than the exception in U.S. stepfamilies.[1] Two-thirds of white remarried mothers have a child by their new husbands.[2] In 1984, one out of five of all children living with their mothers have a half-sibling living at home.[3] Since the number of half-siblings will grow along with that of stepfamilies, an analysis of sibling dynamics in the stepfamily must include an attempt to deal with half-siblings as well.

Relationships between half-siblings are potentially as complex as those of stepsiblings. Since Cinderella is one of our paradigmatic tales about stepsisters, it is worth noting that in the ancient original she was a half-sister. The story is from China and dates from the T'ang Dynasty (618–907 A.D.). In this version, a man has two wives and has a daughter by each of them. One of the wives dies, and the man dies soon after. The daughter of the dead wife must now live with her stepmother and a half-sister. After that point, the outlines of the story are approximately the same as the Western version, except that the heroine has a magical fish to help her, rather than a fairy godmother. But the "first" Cinderella had to struggle against a half-sister, rather than stepsisters, and she has many present-day counterparts.[4]

When a child is born to remarried parents, the stepfamily is transformed. The new child provides a blood link between all family members that was not there before. It would be too simple, though, if the birth of a half-sibling always had the same effect on the other children in a stepfamily. Much depends on previous factors: how many children there were in the stepfamily before, what their ages were, what the relationship between the parent and stepparent was like, and the relation between the stepparent and the stepchildren. To explore why and how these factors produce different outcomes, three case studies follow. The first illustrates a family where there had been an only child before the mutual child was born. The second describes one where there were two brothers before the birth. And in a third family, we look at the point of view of the half-sibling himself.

### The Singers: An Only Child Gets a Half-Sibling

The Singer family is a simple stepfamily living in a suburb of New York City. Rose Singer has a twenty-four-year-old daughter, Patty, from a previous marriage. Rose and Seymour, her present husband, have a son, Jason, who is ten years old. Seymour met Patty when she was 4, but he and Rose did not marry until Patty was about 10. Patty's father and mother had divorced several months before Rose first met Seymour. Jason was born about three years after Seymour and Rose's marriage, and his arrival was not welcome to Patty. Rose said of Patty's behavior at the time, "She was embarrassed that I was pregnant. There were a lot of jealous, competitive feelings. When Jason was an infant was the time when it really got out of hand. She was running away from home, I don't mean very far, but she was running back and forth going to her father, and she decided she wanted to live with her father. That lasted two weeks. She was fourteen." Although Patty's anger subsided, it is still present, and manifests itself continually, in spite of the amount of time that has passed, and the fact that Patty is twenty-four: "[She shows] anger, not so much towards Jason but criticizing the way we bring him up. She still does. We 'let him get away with too much,' we 'can't handle him.' "

Separate interviews were conducted with the parents and each of the children. At the time of the interviews, the four Singers lived in a compact apartment. Patty and Jason had their own rooms, and Rose and Seymour had a room as well. There was great friction between Patty and Seymour. Rose frequently felt torn between her loyalty to

Patty and her love for Seymour. The grounds for Patty's resentments often varied, but they recurred around two themes; one general and the other specific. The first was her jealousy over her mother's and stepfather's attentions to her half-brother, Jason. The other major issue centered around Patty's sleeping with her boyfriend, Jimmy, and his spending the night in the apartment.

Patty's resentments against her half-brother and stepfather began with a conflict over their moving to a larger apartment after the baby was born.

*Rose:* "We lived in New Jersey when we were married and Jason was born. He did not share a room with us. We had our bedroom and we had one bedroom for Patty. Jason was sleeping in the foyer because the pediatrician did not feel Jason should sleep in our bedroom no matter how young, he would hear noises. Patty was very unhappy about moving. She even said she would give up her bedroom to Jason to stay there. . . . She had a lot of friends, right there in her school and she didn't want to change schools."

*Author:* "Whom was the resentment directed against?"

*Seymour:* "She felt resentment that we were doing this to her. It was a very rough time. Patty had graduated from junior high school and was going to senior high, but all her friends were still there. There is no physical space competition here . . . one of the major things is that Rose and Patty feel that I'm overprotective of Jason. Patty resents it if I say to turn the television down when Jason is going to sleep. While Patty can't admit she wants anything from me, she resents my giving to Jason."

One might wonder why, being 24 years old with a well-paying job, Patty does not live on her own, in light of the resentments she feels. Her explanation reveals a great deal about the dynamics of this particular set of stepfamily and half-sibling relationships. Patty had earlier been engaged to a young man, but had broken it off. While they were engaged, the two of them bought a two-family house. After the breakup, Patty bought the house from her ex-fiance. Although she is the owner of her own house, she claims that she must remain living with the family because the costs of carrying the house are so high that she must rent it out to two families. Were she to live in even one part of the house, she claims, the mortgate payments would be unaffordable. Her assertion is that she must live with Rose, Seymour, and Jason until she gets together enough savings to live on her own. But neither parent nor stepparent accept that.

*Rose:* "She really doesn't want to live in that house. She offered to us that Seymour and I should rent out one of the apartments in the house and not pay the rent she's getting now, to pay this rent, the maintenance here. She would live there."

*Author:* "Are there more than financial reasons for her not moving out?"

*Seymour:* "She's not ready to live on her own. But she doesn't like our standards. There are disagreements about her present boyfriend sleeping over."

Two other items suggest that Patty wants to stay, rather than being obliged to. One is linked to her previous decision to stay with her mother, stepfather, and toddler half-brother when it came time to go to college. Patty said that she wanted to go to college in Arizona, but Seymour and Rose said that they couldn't afford it. Whereupon Patty said, "Well, if I can't go to Arizona, then I'm going to stay right here," and she ended going to a nearby commuter college. This move appears to have been a deliberate calculation, to overshoot in her initial choice so that she would "have to" live at home. The other reason for suspecting that she has no intention of leaving even now is that, when the interviews were conducted, Patty had just spent a considerable amount of money remodelling her room in the Singer apartment!

The main, specific conflict at present is over whether Patty's boyfriend, Jimmy, should spend the night. It was Rose who granted Patty permission for this, but Seymour feels that it is inappropriate, particularly because of its effect on Jason.

*Seymour:* "Because it became such an issue because of me, Rose felt I was breathing down her neck, to the point where I pulled back from the apartment. Rose feared that she would lose Patty. . ."

*Author:* "What is the effect on Jason?"

*Seymour:* "He asks a lot of questions. 'Is he here?' 'Are they fucking?' He is very interested in sex and talks about it quite a bit. . . . His curiosity is heightened. There is a highly sexualized atmosphere."

Patty's having Jimmy sleep over bears directly on Jason's relationship with her. Jason is jealous of Jimmy. He cares deeply about his half-sister, whom he considers a sister, and is hurt by her hostility and cruelty to him.

*Author:* "Do you think she loves you?"

*Jason:* "I'm not sure. When I get a cut or something and say, 'Oh Patty, it hurts,' and my parents aren't home, she doesn't do anything. She's not that much of a caring person."

*Author:* "Do you ever go to Patty if there is a problem?"

*Jason:* "Sometimes when my mother and father are arguing I go to her and talk to her because she's been through a divorce. . ."

*Author:* "Does it bother you when they fight?"

*Jason:* "Sometimes I feel like a marriage counselor, cause I'm always trying to help."

*Author:* "Do you feel responsible?"

*Jason:* "Sometimes."

*Author:* "If you were Emperor of the world, how would you set things up?"

*Jason:* "Jimmy move to Alaska. . . . Wish Patty would care about us more. . . . One time I was lost and she couldn't care less and my parents were worried sick. My parents told me about it. I wasn't really lost."

*Author:* "What kinds of things would you have Patty do?"

*Jason:* "She wouldn't get angry at everything. Not that she has a temper problem, just that she gets angry a lot."

One important point remains to explain Jason's role. Patty has a cat. The cat hates Jimmy. Jason is protective of the cat, and keeps it in his room. If Patty left, and the cat left with her, Jason said, "I would die." The cat has a significance for him that is far greater than its simply being a pet.

What is Patty's perspective in this? Seymour and Rose recall that when they were courting, Patty adored Seymour, but that as soon as they wed, Patty's adoration turned to rage. The central emotion that comes through in her interview is her jealousy of her half-brother and resentment of her stepfather.

*Author:* "Do you remember how you felt when Jason was born?"

*Patty:* "It was bad for my mother . . . my mother didn't have the patience for it. She's very short-tempered. But I didn't feel that way about my little brother and my little sister by my father. . . ."

*Author:* "Do you feel that Jason takes away some of Rose's affection for you?"

*Patty:* "Definitely not! Seymour feels like my mother is always on my side."

*Author:* "Is that true?"

*Patty:* "To a certain extent. . . . If there's an argument between me and Seymour, he feels like he has to get Jason on his side. If I have a fight with Seymour, my mother starts screaming at him, and he'll go talk to Jason about it. Jason is not an adult, but Seymour will tell him what he feels, and Jason becomes like an arbitrator."

*Author:* "Do you feel that Jason has too much power?"

*Patty:* "Definitely. It makes him very unhappy. I don't think he thinks he could cause a breakup [of Seymour and Rose] but he thinks he could hold it together. . . . Jason doesn't want me to move out. I'm not really sure why. Jason feels like he can hold the family together."

Let us step back and review what this drama has to tell us about stepfamilies in general and half-siblings in particular. Patty has an extraordinary amount of power, because she lived with her mother alone for so long that they established a very durable relationship. She had Rose all to herself, her father was at a safe emotional distance, and she still feels very affectionate towards his children, her other half-siblings. Her mother came to depend on her, and it gave her a quasi-adult status far beyond her years. Seymour was no threat as long as he was simply her mother's boyfriend. But his arrival in the home infuriated her, because it undermined her closeness to her mother, broke up the close couple the two of them had formed for so long, and pushed Patty back into a childlike status after so many years as an almost-grownup. The remarriage was followed by the arrival of yet another competitor for Rose's attention and affection—baby Jason. This, in turn, caused a family move that tore Patty loose from social networks that are vitally important in early adolescence. This doubled her rage. Her power is still enormous, because she knows that Rose feels guilty about marrying Seymour and can be manipulated as a result. The proof of this power is her ability to get Seymour, against his wishes (which are partly due to concern for his son and partly a function of his attraction to Patty and competition with Jimmy), to acquiesce in her having her boyfriend sleep over.

Patty wants to hold onto her mother, whom she still regards as her property, as a weapon against Seymour and his ally Jason, whom she treats harshly and coldly. For her to leave would mean giving up the struggle, though staying means giving up the full autonomy and the personal development that most young adults undertake at this stage in their lives. One suspects that the broken engagement is significant in this regard: losing her mother, and the immense power she wields in the Singer family, were too high a price to pay for adulthood and wifehood. Her solution, then, is to keep the status of a quasi-adult, with "her own little empire," as Seymour calls it, even as she remains socially, psychically, and physically entangled in the family.

Jason, too, has immense power, partly in his own mind and partly in reality. He sees himself as responsible for keeping the family to-gether. He is protective of his half-sister, probably feels sexually at-tracted to her, and detests his competitor, Jimmy. But Jason is small, and Jimmy is big. (He is also a police officer and carries a pistol.) So Jason protects Patty's cat instead of protecting his sister. Keeping the cat in his room is a way of keeping his tie to his sister. Jason also feels responsible for keeping his parents together to the point where he talks of himself as a marriage counselor. This feeling of adult status is rein-forced by the fact that his father, on the occasion of fights with Rose, talks to him more as a peer and friend than as a son.

Two salient patterns emerge from this account. The first is that Patty feels that she was betrayed by her mother and is sacrificing much of her life as a young adult in trying to set things right. Jason, on the other hand, is literally at the center of things, and the burden of his part-real and part-imagined power is very heavy on his little ten-year-old shoulders.

### Danny Greco: An Older Brother Gets a Half-Sibling

Danny Greco is a nineteen-year-old college student. His parents, Lucy and Dominic, divorced in 1974 when he was six, and his younger brother, Paul, was two. His mother was awarded custody of the boys, and struggled as a poor single parent until 1980, when she remarried, to Guido Ianello. At the time of the remarriage, Danny was twelve and Paul was eight. Four years later, Lucy and Guido had a son, Larry. Dominic had been living with a girlfriend, Rosa, whom he married around the same time, in 1984; they have no children. Guido Ianello had been married before, briefly, for about a year, but there were no children from that marriage. Both Dominic and Guido are presently truck drivers, but both have worked off and on at different jobs over the years. Lucy had been very hardpressed financially while a single mother; for a while she was on welfare and needed food stamps. She worked in a bank as a teller for several years until Larry was born, and now she is a full time housewife.

Danny gets along well with his father and Rosa, whom he refers to as "my father's wife." He likes his stepfather, whom he calls "Guido," and says that he thinks of him "as a friend." He adores his half-brother, and refers to him as his "smaller brother." He feels that there is something pejorative in the term half-brother. But his feelings about Larry had changed radically.

*Danny:* "I was angry when my mother was pregnant. Because I still kept in touch with my father, and I still loved him, and I loved her too. It was like the final straw, because it meant that there was no chance of reconciliation between them. But then, from the day he was born, things changed really dramatically. I love him with all my heart. It's amazing. It's a totally new thing. Before Larry was born, I thought, 'Well, he's only going to be my *half*-brother.' But once he was born, I always referred to him as my full brother."

*Author:* "Before Larry was born, did you dream of bringing your parents back together?"

*Danny:* "It was a fantasy. I knew it was impossible because they never got along. It was like a dream I knew could never be realized."

*Author:* "And you say your feelings changed after Larry was born?"

*Danny:* "Immediately. From the moment I set eyes on him, I never put him down. I looked in amazement at him. He was like a gift. And at my mother's age, the doctors said it was impossible, and she had to go the hospital for a couple of operations."

Danny was also happy for Guido, because Larry is his only child, Paul, too, was happy, not just about the remarriage but about the birth of Larry. "He was thrilled at the birth from beginning to end. He was looking forward to having another brother. There was no resentment at all."

*Author:* "How did you feel about your mother getting remarried?"

*Danny:* "I wanted her to get remarried. She had dated, and she deserved to have a good marriage. My father put her through a lot of hell. It [the divorce] was all his fault. He was young, and he was more concerned with his own social life. She deserved somebody to take care of her. She had taken such good care of us."

*Author:* "Did you have the feeling that Guido was displacing you as the 'man of the house?' "

*Danny:* "No, I was never in that position, I was never the 'man of the house,' because my mother really took care of us by herself."

Danny's relations with his brother Paul, by his account, are not particularly close.

*Danny:* "Well, we get along. We have separate friends. We shared a room, but we weren't really close. I was never like the older brother who had to approve everything. He used to try to imitate me. I'm artistic, and sometimes I'd find him drawing and painting pictures. We used to listen to the same kind of music, although nowadays he's older, and he knows he doesn't have to copy me. . . . There's a distance. We don't talk over problems with each other, we tolerate each other, and we almost never fight. In a way, the birth of Larry may have kept us closer together than we might otherwise be, because it's something we have in common."

On the other hand, Danny's relations with Larry are remarkably close.

*Danny:* "I feel responsible for Larry. You know, my mother's pushing forty, so she's old. It's hard for her to keep up with a little three year old like that. I wind up taking care of him a lot. I'm a mix between a father figure and an older brother. My stepfather is out of the house more than I am. If Larry cries in the middle of the night, I'm the first person he calls. [This last was said with great pride and satisfaction.]

"So I feel responsible for him. And I feel responsible to my mother. She really had a hard time. I feel like I ought to pay her back, like when I'm older and have a career. I wouldn't tell her now, I'd just go ahead and do it. . ."

At the end of the interview, Danny was explaining just how deep his feeling of "responsibility" toward Larry goes.

*Danny:* "One of the reasons I never went away to school was my feeling of being responsible for Larry. I just can't picture myself out of the house. I would like to see Larry grow up in a real family and live a better life than I did."

Although Danny was "angry" when his mother was pregnant, because it meant that he had to give up the fantasy of reuniting his parents, his description of an instantaneous emotional transformation is so striking that it invites further scrutiny of the sibling world of the Ianello family. Danny's attachment to Larry was formed so abruptly, and is so strong, that we have to suspect that something more is going on. Although he claims that he did not feel displaced by Guido, and is undoubtedly sincere in saying that he likes him like a friend, there seems to be a clear element of competition between him and his step-father. The stakes in the competition may include Danny's mother or power in the household or both, but the most obvious item over which the rivalry has arisen is Larry himself.

What Danny describes as responsibility is much more than that. He has transformed the anger at the situation into an attachment so deep that he is the first person the toddler cries for in the night. He "never put him down." This is partly because his stepfather is out of the house more than Danny is. Thus he describes himself as a combination of "a father figure and an older brother." His attachment to Larry is certainly a warm one, but it is also one in which he wants to replace his stepfather.

Almost as confirmation that his relationship with Larry is much more than fraternal attachment, Danny's relations to his full brother are not close. They were warmer in the past, but he was never an older brother to Paul with the same intensity as with Larry. Indeed, he perceives that Larry may have kept them together more than they otherwise would be now.

Danny's adaptation to the critical event of Larry's birth has been a "positive" one in the sense that he is no longer full of conscious anger, and he has given up the dream of reuniting his parents. But the adaptation has its price. Because of what he calls his feeling of responsibility, he made a major decision not to leave home and go away to college. It is striking that a three-year-old half-sibling could have such a powerful effect on the life of a young man, but this is testimony to the strength of stepfamily ties. Danny has found his place in the new family, but now that he has found it, he does not feel that he can leave it. Remember the nineteen-year-old's own words: "I just can't picture myself out of the house."

## Abraham Frank: The Mutual Child

Abraham Frank is a nineteen-year-old Orthodox Jewish college student in Philadelphia. He lives with his father, Jacob, aged sixty-one,
who divorced his mother five years ago. This was Jacob's second
marriage; he had previously lived in the Eastern Europe, where he was
divorced thirty years ago from a woman named Rachel, by whom he
had three daughters, Deborah, Soshana, and Pnina, now aged thirty-
eight, thirty-seven, and thirty-five, respectively. Abraham did not meet
his half-sisters by this previous marriage until they immigrated to the
United States in the early 1980s. Abraham's mother, Ruth, had been
married to a man named Mordechai before she wed Jacob, by whom
she had had a daughter, Rebecca. Ruth and Mordechai were divorced
twenty-three years ago, and Ruth was Rebecca's single mother from
the time the little girl was four until she was nine. Abraham was born
soon after Ruth and Jacob were married. He was thus brought up in a
household that consisted of his mother, his father, and his half-sister
Rebecca. Since the divorce of his parents, Abraham has lived with
Jacob.

> I always thought Rebecca was my sister. When I was six my Dad explained
> that I had three other sisters, too. At the time I never thought I'd meet
> them. Now I see Deborah and Soshana and Pnina, but I'm formal, very
> formal in these relationships. My father feels very uncomfortable, too, and
> doesn't want to chase after relationships with them.

With regard to his relationship with Rebecca, Abraham says, "Our
histories are different. . . There is some bitterness with my father and
her." Rebecca's situation with Jacob as her stepfather was indeed an
unhappy one. "My mother always said, 'He never liked her. She wasn't
his child.'" Abraham says that apparently her stepfather used to beat
her, but the stories vary regarding how much. Abraham was preferred
over Rebecca because he was his father's son. "My father used to say,
'I'm supporting her. That's enough.'" Rebecca was always excluded
on family trips, but "My father didn't want her around, because she
was not his daughter. She ate, but as far as other necessities, she had
to get them on her own."

The situation was so inequitable, Abraham was so clearly privileged,
and his half-sister ignored and beaten, that there was probably more
animosity on her part than Abraham admits. "There was jealousy,"
says Abraham, "but it levelled out, and I didn't necessarily see it. She
does say I was spoiled." A poignant incident illustrates her point. When

Abraham was ten years old, his father brought him home a train set. Although at the time Rebecca was nineteen years old, she spent the whole day in her room, weeping, crying, "He gets everything."

On the positive side, Abraham introduces her to strangers as "my sister." "She taught me about taking girls out from the girl's perspective, like what do you do with them?" He has a particularly fond memory of the summer of 1983, which he spent being close to Rebecca. "I met my sister and we had a really good time. We talked about girls. I was always striving to be grown up, and Rebecca had to be grown up because my father was not supportive of her."

Although Abraham claims, "It never took that much of a toll," the differing degree of privilege between the two children was apparently too great for their relations to remain cordial, particularly when Rebecca had achieved some degree of autonomy. After Ruth and Jacob divorced, Rebecca had wanted to strike out on her own, but for cultural reasons was obliged to stay with her mother until she married a year later. Two years ago, there was a major confrontation, and Abraham remembers exactly the date and the time. He says that Rebecca's husband "pushed her into anger against my father. She accused me of taking things and lying, of trying to hurt her mother. A lot of resentment against me and my father came out. I don't talk to Rebecca since that time. I represent my father to her and her family."

Rebecca's experience must have been brutal. First, there was the breakup of her parents' marriage; after that she had her mother all to herself for five years. Then suddenly she lost her place: Jacob replaced her as her mother's intimate, and he treated her with hostility. And then she was displaced by another child, her half-brother Abraham, who was treated in princely fashion. Abraham himself was hardly to blame for the favors showered upon him. He does remember his half-sister's resentment, but regards her as his sister, and acknowledges her guidance while he was growing up. But it is not unexpected that eventually Rebecca's long-simmering resentment boiled over, her mother's divorce from Abraham's father notwithstanding.

### And Baby Makes . . . Things Complicated

For older children in stepfamilies, the birth of a half-sibling follows hard on the heels of other major events, including parents' remarriage, the joining of stepsiblings in the new family, and the mother's pregnancy. The rapid succession of such events can make adjustments very difficult. Such a situation is extremely common, since one fourth of remarrying mothers will have a baby by the new spouse within a year of the wedding, and one half will take this step before a year and a half have elapsed.[5]

The implications are serious for the parents as well as the children but for quite different reasons. Our focus here will be on the effects of the birth of a half-sibling to the youngsters in a stepfamily, but as with the other topics discussed in this book, the parents cannot be excluded from the picture.

Whether the parents had children from a previous marriage or not, the new child signifies a decisive step, the assumption of a parental role within the new family, and not just the assumption of a marital role. As Esther Wald points out, one consequence of divorce is that adults relinquish the marital role without giving up the parental role. Thus, upon remarriage to a person with children by a previous marriage, an adult acquires both a new marital role and a stepparental role. In this type of stepfamily, the adult has a parental role (toward his or her children from a previous marriage), a stepparental role (toward the children of the new spouse) and a marital role (with relation to the new spouse). But the parental role is only shared with an ex-spouse, and intimate, regular interaction with such people sharing parenthood is absent.

When a remarried parent has a mutual child with a new spouse, yet another role is added to the picture. A more conventional parental role is acquired, that is, one shared with a spouse. Not only does the addition of yet another role to an already complex picture make things even more complicated, it requires of the adult two types of parental roles, one shared with a present spouse and the other shared with an ex-spouse. The possibilities of role-strain and role confusion are that much greater.

For example, a recent study illustrated role expectations and role performance in stepfamilies with mutual children. Respondents in a southwest American city were asked, "Whose duty is it to care for and bring up children from the prior and the present marriage?" This question was asked with regard to 1. the husband's children from a previous marriage, 2. wife's children from a previous marriage and 3. children from the current marriage. Over half the respondents thought that the husband and wife should have the same responsibility when it came to raising children from the other's previous marriages. But over one third thought it should be "wife more than husband" with regard to her children from a previous marriage, and more than one third thought it should be "husband more than wife" with regard to his children from a previous marriage. Almost 10 percent thought it should be the husband's *exclusive* responsibility to care for children from his previous marriage, and 5 percent thought it should be a wife's exclusive responsibility to care for her children from her previous marriage. However, there was virtually unanimous agreement (95.5 percent) that the husband and wife had the same duty to care for mutual children from their present union. In short, parents of children from previous marriages do not have a unanimous set of role expectations. While there is substantial support for the idea that there is a mutual obligation of parents and stepparents towards the children in their families, there also appears to be a strong bias towards maintaining responsibility along blood lines.

In actual behavior, authority usually does tend to follow blood relations. Respondents were asked, "Who makes decisions about children from different marriages?" For mutual children, husband and wife share equally in decisions for 70 percent of the respondents, and wife more than husband for 27 percent. But in only a minority of the stepfamilies do husband and wife share equally in decisions about children from previous marriages (20 percent for the husband's children from a previous marriage and 29 percent for children from a wife's previous marriage). More than 60 percent of the time, husband "always" or "more than wife" made the decisions with regard to "his" children; the figure was slightly less than 60 percent for wives and "their" children.

The congruence of blood and responsibility produces a role pattern in which mutual children are the focus of both parents' authority, but their half-siblings will tend to only have a single adult, their one biological parent, assuming responsibility for them in the stepfamily. Stepfamilies with both children from previous marriages and children from the present marriage are thus differentiated in ways that are unknown to intact nuclear families. There is a "stratification," a layering, of authority and responsibility that is unique.[6]

When remarried parents have a child in common, they have transformed a couple with legally (and transiently) related dependent children into a biologically related family. *Stepfamilies with a mutual child are fused in a way that stepfamilies without one are not.* The conversion of a remarriage into a biological family has consequences for the stability of the family, the quality of relationships between spouses, for the children, and for the mutual child itself.

Lucille Duberman notices that there was a strong relation between the presence of a mutual child and positive evaluations of the marriage. In her words, "We found that of those [step]families who had had children together, 78 percent rated excellent in their relationships between stepchildren and stepparents, compared to 53 percent of those who did not have children together.[7] The reason for this relation, however, is not clear: does the arrival of a mutual child improve marital relations, or is it a good relationship that tends to lead remarried people to decide to have a child together? Duberman admits that her data do not provide an explanation.

Ten years after Duberman's groundbreaking study, Albrecht pointed out a similar, but less strong, association: "In response to the question comparing the respondents' present marriage with their former marriage, 91 percent of those who have children from the *present union* said the marrige was much better. However, only a somewhat smaller percentage of those without children from the present marrige (86 percent) also rated it much better."[8] Once again, we cannot tell which came first, the better marriage or the birth of the mutual child, though it seems evident that there is some relation between the two.

So much for the parents; how about the siblings? A basic distinction needs to be made between the half-sibling role expectations that accrue to a stepchild, and those that accrue to the position of a mutual child. Both can be called half-siblings, but the content of the two roles is quite distinct. From the very outset, there is a basic "inequality" built into half-sibling relations in stepfamilies. Most of the time, at least one of the half-siblings will have only one biological parent in the family, while the other or others will have two. The child or children with only one biological parent is clearly more "marginal" than the child with both biological parents present. One might expect that this would tend to produce strong resentment against half-siblings. Sometimes this is so, particularly when the older child is an only child. But it has also been found to have the opposite effect.

Duberman discovered a very strong relation between the birth of a half-sibling and the better quality of relations between stepsiblings: 44 percent of the parents who had a mutual child asserted that the relations between the siblings were excellent, whereas only 19 percent of those without mutual children made this statement. Granted, parents are not always aware of what is really going on between siblings and stepsiblings, but parental reporting is often the only source available for ascertaining this information. And the sharpness of the difference between the two figures is arresting enough to be convincing. She adds an interesting quote from a respondent mother: "My children and my stepchildren like each other more since we had the baby. They all adore the baby! I don't think the older children are really pals, but at least they have the baby in common."[9]

This limited evidence would suggest that the addition of a half-sibling is associated with reportedly improved stepsibling relations. Yet better stepsibling feelings may not comprise so much an increase in affection for each other as a focusing of everyone's affection on the new baby. Perhaps the half-sibling does not make stepsiblings like one another more, but it gives them all a common focus of their affection. Duberman also suggests that a dimension of the new stepsibling bond may be a common feeling of jealousy towards the newcomer. And if the half-sibling is born into a stepfamily where there was previously only one child, there will be no one else to share the feelings of jealousy with, and the feeling of being displaced will be stronger than feelings of affection.

One factor that could affect the nature of relations between half-siblings is the age interval between them. In an early essay on the question, Paul Bohannon speculated that, "There is usually a significant age gap between sets of half-siblings, and it seems that there is often a relationship of studied avoidance or formality between them. Sometimes, of course, the older set of half-siblings become important parent substitutes for the younger ones."[10] Perhaps, if there is a small age difference between the half-siblings, the baby will be threatening; if there is a large age difference, there may be greater likelihood that a quasi-parental role can be adopted towards the new arrival.

All of these observations are speculative rather than factual, but they can be summarized as follows. The birth of a mutual child is associated with better marital relations between remarried parents, but it is not clear which causes the other. Better relations between stepsiblings often accompany the birth of a half-sibling, but such amelioration may be due more to shared jealousy and a common focus of affection than to warmer mutual feelings. The age interval between older stepsiblings and the mutual child could be important in that younger children could feel rivalry, whereas older children could feel secure enough to show parent-like care.

The in-depth interviews with adult stepsiblings and the results of the SAA survey indicated distinct types of adaptations to the birth of a half-sibling. In the discussion below the focus is, first, on the negative and then on the positive aspects of a half-sibling's birth for the other stepsiblings. Then we take a look at the half-sibling role of the mutual child itself. The negative aspects of acquiring a half-sibling can be summarized as forms of "betrayal," while the essence of the positive aspect is "renewal." At the center of all this is the new arrival itself, who in literal as well as metaphorical ways is the "hub" of the step-family.

## Betrayal

Rachel, eight years old, expressed a nearly universal feeling among children of remarrying parents.

> When my father got remarried, I felt like, 'Oh, no, they're going to be married—that means my dad won't have a chance to get married to my mother again.' But in a way I was kind of glad for them. It was a woman that he loved, and I'm glad he got married. I saw her before daddy got married to her and she's pretty nice.[11]

The fantasy of reuniting divorced parents is extremely strong among children. It is the psychological counterpart to the narcissistic belief, particularly pronounced among younger children, that they were somehow responsible for the breakup. The feelings of omnipotence that lead to the notion of responsibility have the same origin: the dream that the child who was powerful enough to break up the parents is somehow powerful enough to bring them together again. Children of divorced parents work out elaborate stratagems for bringing parents face to face. A Hollywood situation comedy, *The Parent Trap*, was based in part on this idea. In reality, the ploys are less sophisticated and less amusing. One of the most common is feigned illness or being "difficult" in some other way. The result is to bring the divorced parents into contact with one another to deal with the situation, though their reunion is rarely, if ever, accomplished by the tactic.

For a child in a stepfamily, the dream dies hard. John and Emily Visher point out that whereas in intact families the children often try hard to keep parents together, in stepfamilies the children frequently want to separate the couple. This is not always conscious, but the aim is to arrange a reconciliation of the divorced biological parent. It is a dream that can hang on after divorce and remarriage, and after all the adults have made it clear that there is no going back.[12]

The significance of the birth of a mutual child becomes understandable in this context. If a remarried parent has a child by his or her new spouse, it makes the dream of reuniting the divorced parents that much harder to hold onto. As Troy, age twelve, said, "Well, I don't think I would like it. If my mother had a new baby I wouldn't be too happy, because she's already had two more of them and there's eight now. And having your father love someone else—it would be better if he lived with your own mother."[13] The arrival of a half-sibling is further confirmation that the previous marriage is over, and a living testimony to the futility of the dream. The baby is thus a living "betrayal" of the ex-spouse by the remarried parent.

For older stepsiblings, the half-sibling's birth can appear even more of a "betrayal," because the child is obviously the result of sexual activity between parent and stepparent. From this perspective, the betrayal is threefold. First, there is the remarriage itself, which makes it harder to dream that mother and father might be reunited. Then there is the birth of the half-sibling, who embodies the end of the fantasy, a living obstacle, as it were. Finally, there is the obvious fact that the child's parents are having sexual relations, which emphasizes the biological parent's having forsaken the ex-spouse.

The baby can also pose a threat to the relation between parent and child in a stepfamily. In an earlier chapter, we looked at how feelings of sibling rivalry were affected by the presence of stepsiblings. The rivalry felt towards a half-sibling is unmistakeable, but of a different texture. The fears of Rachel, age eight, about her remarried mother having a child describe the problem.

> I don't think I would like it. I would wake up at midnight and hear crying. I wouldn't get enough sleep. I have this friend named Alexandra who has a little sister, and it's like her sister gets more attention. She feels like that and I'd feel like that. Whenever her little sister puts half her toe in Alexandra's room, Alexandra will scream at her and say, 'Get your foot out of my room!' In some ways I don't think Alexandra treats her sister really good. I'll start playing with her little sister and I'll tickle her and make her laugh and Alex will say, 'Don't play with her. You came to play with me, not her.' And she'll make both of us feel bad about it.[14]

Rachel's fears are based on her perception of Alexandra's jealousy. Her friend feels threatened by a half-sister's incursion into her space and by her feelings of competition with her half-sister over attention shown by Rachel.

Thirty years ago, Podolsky pointed out how sibling rivalry is compounded with regard to a half-sibling, because the newborn has two biological parents, compared to its half-sibling's one.[15] Podolsky was describing stepfamilies formed primarily from bereavement, and most stepchildren with half-siblings today do have a second living parent somewhere. But that second parent is still physically distant, and is likely to be remarried, probably also a stepparent, and a parent of a mutual child by a new spouse. Though still living, the absent parent is thus not an everyday presence for the stepchild the way both parents of the half-sibling are.

One of the young adults interviewed echoed Rachel's feelings. She had mentioned that she was deeply disturbed by the birth of her half-sister. The author asked, "Can you talk about why your half-sister's birth bothered you so?" Her response was,

> Well, I was my father's favorite and everything, and like now she was born . . . and it got worse, because my father would tell me, 'Oh, how could you be doing this, when she grows up she'll never do that.' I think he sincerely believed that he was going to bring her up great and his new wife would be so much a better mother than my mother, but [my half-sister] would never have the problems, like, go through some of the things I went through.

Thus, the fears of being displaced do not necessarily abate as the children grow up. Adult children can feel as threatened by a half-sibling's rivalry as can young stepchildren. Roosevelt and Lofas quote a young man, both of whose parents married new spouses who had not had children, and who had new children after remarrying. He was discussing his half-siblings:

> It wasn't really the marriage itself. . .it was the fact that they had children. That's where it breaks down. I felt alienated from those kids. My sister and brother, all of us, were jealous of them. I don't like little kids anyway. I guess I'm sort of rude. I say, 'Would you pop him in the oven?' and stuff like that. I don't know if I would lift a finger to help either of my stepmother's kids if they were in trouble. My brother, who's in college, fantasizes about getting rid of them totally."[16]

Brenda Maddox tells an anecdote about her own adult stepson that also illustrates how fears of a new baby can persist even when stepsiblings grow up. She had seen her stepson off to college, and six weeks later gave birth to his half-brother. She and her husband had heard nothing from the college student in the intervening time, but just as the baby was born, he just "happened to be passing by the hospital" and decided to come up to visit. "When the boy finally did get to see me the next day, he asked the question, which had propelled him two hundred miles, at the critical moment. 'Are you,' he said, nodding in the direction of the sleeping baby, 'going to give him my room?' "[17]

Visher and Visher point out factors that can increase or diminish the feelings of jealousy inspired by a half-sibling. In a situation where one of the adults in a stepfamily has not had children previously, the accession to parenthood can produce a concentration of attention on the mutual child that can easily be perceived as taking away from the other children. But if both parents have had children by previous marriages, the arrival of a stepsibling is not as traumatic. The children in the family have already been sharing the home with stepsiblings, and have had to share a parent as well. A new arrival does make for changes, but it is not as likely to be seen as competing with the stepchildren for affection.[18]

Another factor that can alleviate feelings of rivalry is the period of time elapsed between remarriage and the birth of the new child. As Griffith, Suchindran, and Koo suggest, the longer the interval between remarriage and the half-sibling's birth, the more likely other children will adjust. Age interval between stepchild and mutual child may thus be important.[19]

Statements by respondents in the SAA survey show how age, and the related hierarchy problems dealt with earlier in the book, seem to play an important role in determining what half-sibling relationships will be like. Of course, these observations must be regarded as of limited value, particularly on this issue, because the respondent parents, at the birth of the child, were probably full of hope and joy. These emotions may have affected their perception of darker feelings among the other children.

The simplest and most straightforward account was as follows.

> My husband had a fourteen-year-old son, and I had two sons, ages ten and twelve when we married nineteen years ago. We together have a son, who is now age seventeen. My kids saw very little of their father and felt a lot of resentment towards their half-brother, probably less towards their stepbrother, who they saw little of. The major problem for them, I think, was my attention being on the new baby and the new husband.

This is probably the simplest statement of the situation, since the siblings are all of the same sex and the stepbrother evidently does not live with them. Loss of place to the new spouse and the half-brother, when previously there had been a monopoly over mother's attention and affection, seem to be the basic elements of the conflict.

What of stepfamilies where there are stepsibling relations as well as half-sibling relations? One stepmother described the reactions of the siblings as differing because of age and blood. Her stepson was fourteen when his half-brother was born. "He was *very* upset, not at all pleased. He tended to be quite hostile." But her own oldest son "was aged twelve. He was ostensibly *very* happy. He was very protective. When he went away to camp when the baby was eight months old, he was very excited to get back and see him. He is still close to him and concerned about him." However, her own youngest son was age eleven and "*very* jealous. He had been the baby since his birth and felt quite ambivalent. But he is also very fond of him and fairly close to him now. This son is now married, with an eight-month-old baby daughter, whom his half-brother is close to. He is also close to his wife. This son had the most evident problems with his stepfather, whom he had been quite close to until the birth of his half-sib, at which time the stepfather withdrew to some extent. This boy then became angry and troublesome and took some of his anger out on his half-sibling.'' The youngest seems to have felt a straightforward resentment at loss of place in the age hierarchy. The respondent's oldest did not feel threatened, perhaps because he was still the oldest in his side of the parallel birth hierarchy. The stepson felt very threatened; this may have been because his connection to the family was via his father, rather than his mother, and he may have felt he was in a more tenuous position.

A clue to understanding the thought processes of children in this predicament is illustrated by the account of another stepmother.

> The oldest boy [the respondent's stepson] was happy in anticipating the birth [of his half-brother] and was delighted that the baby was a boy. He shows great affection and protective attitudes towards his younger [blood] brother. (I view this is a typical sibling relationship.) At the birth of the baby, however, the oldest boy indicated that his natural mother would then become the stepmother of the baby, just as I had become his stepmother when marrying his father! He now understands why this is not the case.

The new arrival was acquiring a coveted position in the family—that of being the youngest and of being more connected than his half-brothers. The boy's fantasy was that he would somehow be required to share his natural mother with the half-sibling, by having her become stepmother to him. The fantasy was not ''true''—although most readers will be obliged to stop and think and wonder if there was any formal family relationship at all between the natural mother of the oldest boy and his half-brother by another mother. But more important was that the boy imagined loss of preeminence in the family. He was a stepson whose membership in the family was by way of his father, and his natural mother was elsewhere. There may be a greater tenuousness for such a child, and the appearance of a half-sibling may consequently be more frightening.

Another parent said,

> The youngest child had the most difficult time adjusting to the birth of the new baby. [The youngest was four years old at the time.] It was the same sex, and he felt displaced in his stepfather's affection. The two middle children (twin girls) were ten at the time the youngest was born and were thrilled with the prospect of having an addition to 'play' with and mother. The oldest child seemed excited but quickly lost interest and spent less time

in our household for six months or so. Now that the youngest is a toddler, he often takes him places and again spends time with him.

It appears from this that, other things being equal, the greater the age difference at the time of the half-sibling's birth, the safer this event will seem to the child.

Other things, though, are never equal. The next response from the survey suggests other important dynamics are at work. The stepmother answered the questionnaire, "We have a unique situation. My husband has been married three times, and has children by all three wives." As for the reaction of the oldest child, by the husband's first marriage, "I don't know his reaction, he didn't have a lot of contact with his dad or the half-siblings until recently." As for the second oldest, by the husband's second marriage, "He's really a quiet child. He doesn't express himself a lot. But a month after our boy was born, he managed to get consent from his mom to come live with us. He's twenty-one now, and really spoils our son." The third oldest child is also by the husband's second marriage. She is a daughter, and "A little competition exists there, although she's nine years older." And finally, the fourth oldest, by the husband's third marriage: "He was living with us at the time [of the half-sibling's birth]. "He really missed his other brother and sister [who were living with his biological mother] and welcomed the baby as a 'real' brother. Still even though the fourth is sixteen, he takes good care of him (the baby). It's interesting, too, because the fourth really likes moving from fourth position to baby (in his other family) and back."

The first child seems to have been somewhat distant, but reduced his distance since the birth of his half-sibling. There is probably a causal link here, for reasons we will look at below. The second child seems to have been so profoundly affected by the birth of his half-brother that he asked to leave his own biological mother so that he could join in the family with the new addition. We do not know the details about his life in the other family, but it does appear that there must have been something quite attractive about the respondent's family as a result of the half-sibling's arrival. The third oldest child reveals signs of the feelings of displacement we have already looked at. This may partly be because she is of a different sex, and partly because her anomalous position as one of two middle children may have been exacerbated by the addition of yet another child to the crowd. Perhaps the "fourth" is the most fortunate in this array. Though he was displaced by his half-brother as the youngest in the respondent's family, he could maintain his "baby" status in his mother's family, enjoying the best of both worlds!

Thus, resentment and fear of competition are by no means the only reaction felt by youngsters to the birth of half-siblings. After all, even in intact families, when there are negative feelings toward a new arrival, the feelings are not unalloyed. In the words of Lamb and Sutton-Smith, "Usurpation of the first-born's unique status in the family sets the stage for resentment and rivalry, but although conflict between siblings is frequent, it usually occurs in the context of generally positive relationships between siblings."[20] Reactions of half-siblings to the newborn can take place in a generally positive atmosphere because, in spite of its ending the dream of reuniting divorced parents and bringing the need to share attention, affection, and space with yet another child, the birth signifies a milestone in the reconstruction of the family; it is a sign of renewal.

### Renewal

Positive feelings stepchildren have about the birth of a half-sibling center around its signaling that they now belong to a "real" family. Prior to the event, children may be inclined to see the remarriage as a temporary arrangement, even when sanctified by religion, codified in law, and established over time. Children, logically, often think of a "real" family as one that is constituted by parents having children together. A stepfamily does not conform to this image and has that much less legitimacy.[21]

For some children, the desire to participate in the family can apparently take precedence over possible competition. Cindy, age eleven, illustrates this point. "I think I really would prefer it now if my mother had a kid. I really like younger kids a lot and if she had a child, it would be like I have to take care of it. It wouldn't be as if she was a sister. It would be like she was a niece or something. . ."[22]

The key to understanding the positive feelings that children often have about the birth of half-siblings is that a half-sibling provides a biological bond to the whole family. The mutual child is a living link that binds all family members together, because it is biologically related to all of them. As the Vishers say, "Now there is a biological family unit within the stepfamily household. . . . Many parents in stepfamilies report the pleasure that their children felt when a baby was born into the family."[23]

Statements by parents from the SAA survey support the Vishers' observation. One mother who has a fourteen-year-old son by a previous marriage reports that when her second son was born to her and her new husband, the boy's reaction was, "Totally positive! He shared in the caring for the baby, in changing his pants, etc. But he realized that the baby would be too young to be a playmate for him."

Then, of course, a half-sibling, in addition to being related by blood to everyone in the family, is a baby, and does not take sides the way adults and stepsiblings sometimes do. A mother whose seven-year-old daughter was five when her half-sister was born "was thrilled and wanted to hold her and play mommy, etc." And again, a stepmother talks of the reactions of her daughter and son:

> Jeannie was age ten when her half-brother was born. She welcomed Billy, but remained somewhat distant at first. As she got to know him, she'd help change his diapers and hold him. By the time he was around three months, she would genuinely say, 'He's so cute!' He's six months now, and she'll hold him or play with him occasionally, but she remains more interested in friends and clothes! Jerry was age eight when his half-brother was born. Jerry enjoys carrying Billy and showing him to friends. He has fed Billy several times and often is the first one to go to Billy when he cries. He seems adjusted well to sharing his dad and stepmom with Billy.

A mother with eleven- and thirteen-year-old sons said of their reaction to the birth of their half-brother, "The boys were very excited— they have two *other* half-brothers who live with their dad. They were pleased to have one live with them. Partly because they already had half-brothers, they knew what to expect." Experience seems to help children get used to half-siblings. This same respondent went on to make an astute observation about such adjustment: "It is . . . my observation that half-sibs tend to pull a stepfamily together, if the parents are relatively non-neurotic. The birth of half-sibs in very neurotic families . . . tend to pull the adults closer, but usually one of the older half-sibs leaves, either physically or by going crazy, substance abuse, etc." The renewing role of a half-sibling, judging by this insight, depends on other factors, such as the emotional preconditions of the family. Whether it is seen as betrayal or renewal may depend on the pre-adjustment of adults and children.

The role of the half-sibling also probably depends on the age and sex of the other youngsters. One mother wrote, "My daughters were excited and spent a great deal of time helping me. They were fifteen and eleven at the time. My stepson who was eleven showed very little interest and my stepdaughter, who doesn't live with us, and was nine at the time, didn't acknowledge his birth at all." It might appear from this that, controlling for the sex of the half-sibling, the younger the child the more ambivalent the feelings, although it is not easy to tell, since the child who apparently denied the event is not a permanent resident in the household.

Another stepmother's response suggests that a nonresident child can be just as ambivalent about the newborn as a child who lives with the stepfamily in question.

> The sister was overjoyed when my daughter, Denise, was born. She was a responsible thirteen year old, came to stay each weekend, and enjoyed caring for the baby. We left Denise with her, before we ever tried a baby-sitter. When my stepdaughter was fifteen she showed the first signs of wanting Daddy more to herself, came over rarely, and had little patience with Denise. This totally reversed when she turned sixteen. She and Denise speak on the phone regularly, she comes over to our house about every other week. The two girls adore each other. Denise's brother was sixteen when she was born. He was disappointed that she was a girl, was awkward with an infant and was somewhat disinterested. He moved in with us (me, the stepmother, his father, and Denise) when Denise was almost two years. They fought a great deal initially, but they are close now. He gets fed up with her, but is also very protective of her.

As in the previous case, it seems that when the half-siblings are more or less the same age, the half-sibling's sex can play a role in his or her reaction. Both children are ambivalent, but it may be easier for her half-sister to accept Denise because she does not have to share the home with her. By contrast, it would appear that the boy has considerable animosity for his toddler half-sibling: for a sixteen-year-old boy to fight "a great deal" with a child less than two, there must be a lot of simmering resentment.

Age, in and of itself, is probably not the important factor leading to feelings of jealousy about the birth of a half-sibling. The emotional complex that may be associated with age is the fear that the new arrival will push the half-sibling out of the picture. Often this does depend on the age, with less feelings of anxiety the older the child, but other factors enter in. As one stepfather responding to the SAA survey said,

> For the daughter who was fifteen at the time of birth of the half-sister, it was a time of fear (fear of displacement and loss) and fear of knowing how to take care of a baby. In three years, these problems have been sorted out and the bond between the two girls is strong. For the daughter who was nine (youngest) at the time of birth of the half-sister, it was a happy thing and she was very close to the baby. Over time, problems started to crop up as the nine year old began to feel displaced by her younger half-sister. These problems have been addressed and are partially resolved. I don't think they will be fully resolved for a long time to come.

One of the respondents argued that what is important in making a child accept a half-sibling's birth is the relationship of the child to his or her stepparent.

> There is one child from the wife's previous marriage, a nine-year-old girl. As an only child she always wanted a sibling and was thrilled at the birth of a baby girl one year ago. She made two comments before the baby's birth, 'I'll be the only one with a different last name,' and 'The baby will be lucky to live with her father.' Since the baby's birth an occasional comment is made about how much attention the baby gets, but I think a full (natural) sibling would complain about that. The older child does not want the baby called her 'half-sister.' She considers her a full sister. She's an easygoing, generous child anyway, so the new baby was not too stressful for her. It's important to mention that the relationship between the older child and her stepfather is excellent. He treats her like his own daughter. This is the key to a good half-sibling relationship.

There are clearly some elements of jealousy here, but with the additional factors of a good stepfather-stepdaughter relationship, a fairly large age gap between the children and a basically easygoing nature, they appear to be manageable.

As with so many aspects of stepfamilies, there are complex layers in the emotional texture of even such a positive reaction as renewal. Consider, for instance, the SAA survey statement of a stepfather with three stepsons ages twelve, ten, and nine, and a daughter by the boys' mother age two:

> All three boys were thrilled with their sister. She is spoiled by all of them. The oldest babysits for her. The youngest boy cleans up her room and puts away her toys. [But then the respondent goes on] The good part about my having a baby with my wife is that I experienced such a feeling of loss after my divorce. I felt like I had lost my only child to a bitter ex-wife who did everything she could to stop me from seeing my son. It didn't work, but it was a hell of a battle. Now that I have a child living with me full time, I feel my ex-wife can no longer threaten me. It's not like if she moves away I'll be left with another man's sons, but I'll have my own daughter all the time to care for.

The half-sibling toddler is evidently accepted and tenderly treated by her stepbrothers. As far as the father is concerned, things are more complex, and the child may be thought of as a bulwark against defeat and desertion. It might even be said that in a way the little girl has been taken hostage. Half-siblings have a central role in the rebirth of the stepfamily, but this role carries with it responsibilities as well as the privilege of being the center of attention.

## The Hub

This observation leads us to look at the position of the new half-sibling. We know that it is associated with positive feelings on the part of the spouses. We know that it can inspire feelings of resentment and competition among older siblings and stepsiblings, particularly stepsiblings linked to the family by their father. We know that it can also pull stepsiblings closer to one another and to the family. The half-sibling is related by blood to everyone and is at the center of the stepfamily. This position has its advantages, but it also has considerable responsibilities and dangers.

The birth makes a stepfamily more "real" because the parents have a child in common. The child is a baby and does not take sides. Part of what gives this baby all this significance is the fact that it is the only person who is related by blood to all of the members of the stepfamily. This has led some to talk of the mutual child as the "hub" of the family, at the center of the spokes of the wheel.

In this way, the mutual child as half-sibling signifies a unique social role, one with important and interesting characteristics. First, it may not be as closely based on biological relatedness as may seem at first sight. Consider, for example, the case of the Isphording family. Judy Isphording is the mother of a son and a daughter, and three years ago she married a man who has five children. There is also a newborn (Katie) in the family. Judy Isphording reports that all the children in the family love Katie, because she is related equally to everyone. She is the "hub of the wheel." But the interesting thing about Katie is that she is adopted. Katie is apparently the hub of the wheel, not because she is related to everyone in the family but because she is related to *nobody* in the family.[24]

Although it would be unwise to discount the biological element in the unifying effect of half-siblings, it must be recognized that what seems to be important in this is not necessarily that the child shares genetic material with everyone equally, but that it shares kinship with everyone in equal degrees. The degree of this kinship may be 50 percent or it may be zero. What is essential is that it be equal.

One of the respondents in the SAA survey provides a variation on this perspective. A stepfather asserted that "Both half-brothers were adopted at birth, and in both cases the children assimilated the new sibling into the family eagerly. Conflicts are not from step-relationships." Strictly speaking, of course, there is no blood relationship between the "half-brothers" and their half-sibling. The adoption provided them both with an equal base line of no blood relationship to the parents or to the newborn. The newborn in this case does, of course, have a blood relationship to the remarried parents, but the relationship between the siblings is an "equal" one, and this may explain the apparent family harmony. Once again, the important factor in reducing the conflict produced by a half-sibling's birth may be the equal degrees of blood relationship shared or not shared.

Moreover, the role of hub half-sibling is one with great power and responsibility. It is a unifying role whose significance is not lost on the child. Very soon the child comes to realize the extent to which it is not only the center of attention in the family, but also the person who pulls the family together. Remember that Jason Singer refers to himself as a "marriage counsellor" (at the age of ten) and that if his sister Patty left the family, taking the cat with her, he would "die." This responsibility may be too much for the child to bear. As Whiteside and Auerbach put it,

> The danger of this position, similar to the role of 'baby' of the family, comes if the child must always be happy—any disturbance reflects on the picture of the new marriage . . . if the role is too rigid, the child receives much nurturance, but must pay for it by continually being cute and adorable.[25]

The power attached to the position of the hub is great enough to be difficult to bear. But even more daunting is the task of fulfilling the role in the event that the parents of the mutual child redivorce. As we saw in the introductory part of this book, the possibility of redivorce is at least as great as the likelihood of divorce in intact families. To any child in divorce, particularly a young child, there is often the feeling that he or she was at least partly responsible for the breakup. For the half-sibling hub child, this feeling of guilt and blame can be that much greater. The child's power *is* greater than that of others, and while no reasonable person can blame a couple's breakup on their child, from the child's point of view he or she will have failed, at least in part, in the responsibility for keeping the family. When the remarried family with a mutual child collapses, it tears the hub of the wheel apart at the same time.

Samantha Bellingham is mother to Laura, age four, and stepmother to Gretchen, age twelve. Gretchen is the daughter of Samantha's husband and his ex-wife. That marriage has been a remarriage that had formed a combination stepfamily in which Gretchen was the hub to two sets of stepchildren. Thus Samantha is both stepmother and mother to hub daughters. She was interviewed, not only for her practical insights into the lives of the two girls, but because she is a family therapist with a thriving practice.

Both Gretchen and Laura, according to her observation, are under a lot of pressure, because they are hubs. Both are "extremely family-oriented," each having a fairly extensive network of stepsibling and half-sibling relations. Samantha says that "There is no one they would rather see than other family members."

For her part, "Gretchen was very conscious of the fact that in the previous family, she was the only one related by blood to everyone. For her, it was particularly difficult when her parents broke up, because there was a breakup of her sets of stepsiblings as well." She is very close to her half-siblings by her father, the children whom her father had brought into the marriage with her mother, partly because the divorce was a bitter one and had the effect of pulling the biological sets of children together with each other, although opposed to their stepsiblings. Gretchen was allied with her father's children, rather than her mother's children.

Although we might expect it, she has given no indication that she feels that the divorce was her fault. "In fact," said Samantha, "she knows that she kept the marriage together longer than it would have otherwise. The pressure for Gretchen comes from seeing her biological parents not get along." In fact, they hardly communicate. She also feels pressure from the fact that when she visits her mother and her half-siblings by her mother, they do not know the details of her everyday life, so that she has to explain and describe things to them that intimates are aware of. But particularly important is the fact that she wants all of her half-siblings to get along, but they do not. Samantha quoted Gretchen as recently saying, "The day I get married, I'm inviting them all to the wedding, and they better all come and they better all be nice to each other." The wish to pull everyone together comes out strongly in that declaration, and perhaps Gretchen suffered as little as she seems to have because she has the good fortune to have a stepmother who is a family therapist well versed in stepfamily issues.

Laura is now in a situation similar to that of Gretchen in the previous marriage. She is in a privileged position, because she is the focus of even more attention than the youngest would get in most other families. Her stepsiblings and half-siblings are all considerably older than she, and they often assume a quasi-parental role. Even Gretchen displays little or no animosity, in part because of her greater age and in part because Samantha took great pains to give Gretchen the feeling of being a helper and participant in the pregnancy and birth.

She also appears to have the inordinate influence associated with the position of hub. "Laura forces me to do things," said Samantha.

> She *forces* family parties. At age 4, she fills the house with people. She invites half-siblings and stepsiblings over to the house, and invites herself over to their house. She always invites them to stay over, but doesn't ask my permission, because she feels that they are all members of the family. She does ask permission when it comes to inviting friends. She totally feels she is calling the shots.

It is difficult to imagine a description that would more clearly depict the control exercised by a toddler at the center of a stepfamily.

Laura has pressure and power, while Gretchen has pressure without power. One is an ex-hub and the other is still the hub; neither role is a familiar one to siblings in conventional families. This observation brings us to the point where we can sum up the characteristics of half-sibling relations.

### Conclusion: Half-Sibling Stages and the Effects of Age

In the case studies presented at the beginning of this chapter, both Danny Greco and Patty Singer were angry during their mother's pregnancy with the half-sibling. In the Frank family, it is possible that Rebecca, too, felt anger when her mother was pregnant with Abraham, but she was not the focus of that interview. The anger, in two out of the three cases, was associated with feelings of betrayal. Patty claimed her anger was because, "It was bad for my mother. My mother didn't have the patience for it." Danny was more candid when he said, "It was like the final straw, because there was no chance of reconciling them."

Immediately after the birth of his half-brother, Danny says, his feelings changed. This did not happen with Patty. Perhaps the explanation for the difference lies in the different sibling constellations of the two children. For Danny, the betrayal symbolized by his mother's pregnancy was relatively simple, because he had already had to share her affection with his younger brother. It thus meant only that he had to give up the dream of uniting his divorced parents. But for Patty, the pregnancy symbolized a double betrayal, as it were. Not only did it mean that her stepfather was there to stay, it meant that she was no longer the only child in the family—there was yet another person to command her mother's attention. This was too great a shock considering her earlier monopoly over her mother, and she seems to have been incapable of moving beyond the feeling of betrayal.

Danny Greco moved beyond a feeling of betrayal to one of renewal, in part because he was previously not an only child. His feeling of renewal and behavior towards his half-brother, however, is complicated. Although he disavows any jealousy of his stepfather, and denies that Guido displaced him as the "man of the house," he clearly enjoys the quasi-parental role he has taken over with the three year old. He points out that his stepfather is out of the house more than he himself is, he is proud of the fact that the little one calls Danny's name first, and says that not only did he avoid going away to college because of his feeling of "responsibility," but cannot imagine himself out of the house. There is unquestionably some element of competition with Guido, which Danny is dealing with by partially taking over the role of father to the child. Clearly Danny's adaptation is more successful than Patty's, in the sense that he has moved beyond hostility, but it is also evident that he is so emotionally entangled that it is hard for him to think of leaving.

Betrayal and renewal can thus be thought of as stages through which stepchildren successfully adapt to the appearance of a half-sibling. Thinking of them as stages permits us to envision their reactions as normal, and to anticipate that children can expect, and be expected, to move from one to the other. However, moving from one to the other may be more difficult for some children than for others, and some may need professional counseling to do so. Even when the transition has been made, emotions are still at work that are more complex than those ordinarily displayed by older, full-blood siblings.

As for the mutual child himself, he is a half-sibling, too, but has a distinctly different role—that of the hub. Let us sum up the characteristics of that role. The hub is in a privileged position. There is the attention and affection usually reserved for the youngest in any family, but a mutual child is in an even more privileged status because he is related to everyone in the family by blood. In this sense, he automatically has a more central position among the youngsters than any of his half-siblings. They are related to only one parent by blood, while he is related to both.

The hub is in a position of power. Laura Bellingham, by Samantha Bellingham's description, has a great deal more control over the adult half-siblings, stepsiblings, stepparent, and parent, than do most four year olds. Not all children are capable of dealing with this age-inappropriate power. As yet we do not know what the long-term psychological effects of the half-sibling role are, but they should be studied. A hub child is, as it were, in a narcissistic heaven, where the adult world is in many ways at the child's beck and call. Giving up a such feeling of omnipotence may be particularly difficult for a half-sibling.

The hub is also in a position of pressure. Rightly or wrongly, a hub can see himself as central to the cohesion of the family. Gretchen was aware, Samantha says, of how important she was to keeping her parents together as long as she did. The desire to unite her stepsiblings and *make* them be nice to each other comes through touchingly. The hub's half-sibling position is also, consequently, a precarious one. The success rate of combination stepfamilies with a mutual child is not particularly high.[26]

In sum, the mutual child's half-sibling role is privileged, pressured, powerful, and precarious. It is difficult, in an exploratory study such as this, to do more than describe the role; the process whereby children adapt to it must be reserved for future study.[27]

The half-sibling role of the mutual child is different from the half-sibling role of the stepchildren in the family. On the basis of the case studies and the survey of the Stepfamily Association of America, it is possible to suggest a tentative hypothesis about what the family effects of this role may be.

To the extent that the half-sibling is born when the stepchildren are very young, the relationships between the children will approximate those of blood siblings. One SAA survey respondent provided an illustration.

> Our kids don't think of each other as a half-brother or -sister. A cousin told my son that he wasn't a real brother, he was a half-brother to the other youngster. My son got real indignant and told his half-brother about it. He told the little one that he was his brother, not to worry about it.

Conversely, to the extent that the half-sibling is born when the stepchildren are in puberty or older, they will adopt a quasi-parental role toward the child. It is in the middle periods that the possibility of antagonism or maladaptation will persist. Stated slightly differently, the likelihood of trouble is lower when children are very small or quite grown up, while the likelihood of dysfunction grows between these two points. The hypothesis suggests a sort of parabola, whose low points are in infancy and puberty; the curve rises while a child is a toddler and may reach an apogee in midlatency, declining in pre-puberty.[28]

Neat as the hypothesis thus sounds, it is obvious that there are complicating factors. One is the tangible effect of whether the stepchild was an only child or not. Another is the effect of whether there are two sets of stepchildren or one. Yet another is the unquantifiable but crucial variable comprising the quality of marital relationship, and the quality of relationship between stepparent and stepchild and between parent and stepchild. There are probably other factors as well. Nonetheless, this parabolic hypothesis may provide a framework for future inquiries into the nature of half-sibling relations.

## Notes

1. Her comments, above, were quoted in *Ms.*, (February 1985): 49.
2. Janet Griffith et al., "Childbearing and Family in Remarriage," unpublished paper, Center for Population and Urban-Rural Studies, Research Triangle Institute, Research Triangle, North Carolina, October, 1983, p. 19.
3. Larry Bumpass, "Some Characteristics of Children's Second Families," *American Journal of Sociology* 90 (November 1984):608–23.
4. Ai-Ling Louie, *Yeh-Shen: A Cinderella Story from China* (New York: Philomel, 1982).
5. Griffith et al., 1983, "Childbearing," p. 19.
6. Jean Giles-Sims, "The Stepparent Role: Expectations, Behavior, and Sanctions," *Journal of Family Issues* 5 (March 1984):116–30.
7. Duberman, 1973, *Stepkin Relationships*, p. 288.
8. Albrecht et al. 1983, *Divorce*.
9. Duberman, 1973, *Stepkin Relationships*, emphasis added.
10. Paul Bohannon, "Divorce Chains, Households of Remarriage, and Multiple Divorces," in P. Bohannon ed., *Divorce and After* (New York: Doubleday, 1968).
11. Dorriet Kavanaugh ed., *Listen to Us! The Children's Express Report* (New York: Workman Publishing, 1978), p. 80.
12. John Visher and Emily Visher, "Common Problems of Stepparents and their Spouses," *American Journal of Orthopsychiatry* 48 (April 1978): 252–261, esp. 260.
13. Kavanaugh, 1978, *Listen to Us!*
14. Ibid., p. 80–81.
15. Edward Podolsky, "The Emotional Problems of the Stepchild," *Mental Hygiene* 39 (June 1955):49–53, esp. 53.
16. Roosevelt and Lofas, 1976, *Living in Step*, p. 151.
17. Maddox, 1976, *Half-Parent*, p. 121.
18. Visher and Visher, 1975, *Stepfamilies*, p. 178.
19. Griffith et al., 1983, *Childbearing*, p. 21.
20. Lamb and Sutton-Smith, 1982, *Sibling Relationships*, p. 5.
21. My thanks to Ms. Joan Holub, a social worker at the North Shore Child and Family Guidance Center in Roslyn, Long Island, for describing this to me.
22. Kavanuaugh, 1978, *Listen to Us!* p. 181.
23. John Visher and Emily Visher, "Children in Stepfamilies," *Psychiatric Annals* 12 (September 1982):832–41, esp. 841.

24. Glenn Collins, "Remarriage: Bigger Ready-Made Families, *The New York Times*, Monday, 13 May 1983, p. B5.
25. Whiteside and Auerbach, *Can the Daughter.*
26. Booth and White, 1985, *Quality and Stability.*
27. Maureen Appel, a family counselor in Roslyn, Long Island, suggests that there are significant parallels between the role of the hub and the role of the only child.
28. Scarr and Grajek, 1982, *Similarities and Differences.*

# 6

# Conclusion: The Sociology of Stepsiblings

*You just don't understand how complicated
our family is!*
—Client, quoted by Esther Wald

### Dynamics of Stepsibling and Half-Sibling Relations

This book is a beginning, and has necessarily been full of tentative, exploratory statements. The four areas chosen for analysis are not the only problematic aspects of stepsibling relations. But sibling rivalry, age order, incest taboos and the birth of a younger sibling are subjects that recur regularly in discussions of children's lives in intact families. Transposing the problems to look at their stepsibling counterparts provides a starting point.

The four areas discussed above have been treated as if they were separate issues. In the real life of stepfamilies, the problems of stepsibling rivalry, age-order changes, stepsibling sexuality, and half-sibling relations are not separate from one another. In order to make sense of them for discussion's sake, they have been dealt with as "ideal types," artificially isolated from one another.[1] In each area, intervening factors may mitigate or change the tensions. The most important of these is the age of the youngsters when the stepfamily was formed, but other factors have also surfaced: sex, number of other siblings (if any), length of time spent in a single-parent household. In the course of the book, propositions have been developed about how the factors combine with the sources of tension to produce different patterns of stepfamily behavior.

Let us summarize the main features of each area, and suggest where they may overlap with each other.

### Stepsibling Rivalry

Except in the case of twins, sibling rivalry starts, for an only child, with the birth of a younger child. It is generated by the obligation to

127

share parental love and attention, but goes farther, to include rivalry over symbols of parental love. It gives rise to a second sort of sibling rivalry, according to standards youngsters and their peers devise. Though psychologically an extension of competition over parental love, this sibling-generated rivalry can provide more satisfactory outcomes. Although it is not possible to win in the competition over parental affection—unless a parent really does love one child more than another—it is possible for siblings to win in sibling-generated competitions.

In some ways, stepsibling competition is simpler than sibling rivalry because the items over which it arises—space, money, clothing, friends—usually really are bones of contention. They usually do not, as it were, stand for something else. In this sense, stepsibling rivalry is analoguous to sibling-generated rivalry in the intact family, because an equitable distribution can be arrived at, and the tension can be successfully adjudicated. In other ways, though, stepsibling rivalry is more intractable, because stepsiblings cannot see one another as having the same presumptive claim to parental affection as they.

Pete Gilbert and Brenda Goldberg provided us with an idea of some of the dynamics of stepsibling rivalry. Brenda Goldberg, soon after the formation of the stepfamily, found herself imitating her stepsister Felicity by attempting to incorporate parts of Felicity's character as her own. On the surface, then, this was an apparently harmonious relationship. But looked at more closely, Brenda's quest to be like her stepsister is probably a hopeless and forlorn quest to make her stepmother love her as much as she would have liked her own mother to love her. Ostensibly, Pete and his stepbrother Max endured years of forced and hostile closeness to one another. Overtly, their emotions were antagonistic and they tried to be different from one another. Yet the outcome of their warfare has given each a clear sense of self. By having someone against whom to define himself, each boy carved out a clear identity, each of which is really just close enough to the other to be distinctly different. Golda Cohen showed the obverse of these two outcomes. Thanks to the passage of time and the arrival of the stepsisters at similar stages in life, solidarity could emerge between stepsiblings of the same sex. Stepsibling solidarity may thus be similar to sibling solidarity; in fact, it might be relatively easier to arrive at, since it is less likely than it is for blood siblings to be overshadowed by the memory of childhood resentments.

Most of the negative aspects of stepsibling rivalry lie in structural aspects of combination stepfamilies, and are thus beyond control. One negative outcome is contained in the notion that one set of children is seen (and see themselves) as the invaders while the other set is seen (and see themselves) as the landlords. Space is the item most at issue, but property and privacy are also involved. Much of what produces this outcome is due to circumstances and is less likely to occur if the new stepfamily is established in a new dwelling, although this is practically impossible for less than affluent stepfamilies. The "two-class family" is also a probable outcome in the event of distinct differences in wealth between the stepfamily and that of the absent, visited parent. Even when there is no real financial difference, the noncustodial parent is likely to be indulgent and generous because of the relative rarity of the visits. Parent and stepparent can do very little to equalize this sort of competition. Competition over parental and stepparental affection is probably similarly intractable, because equal treatment of all children by both parent and stepparent contains within it a basic injustice; a stepsibling cannot be seen as having the same claim to a child's parent's love as the child himself.

Although such negative consequences of stepsibling rivalry may be built into the system, positive outcomes are also possible. Stepsiblings can provide models of identification for one another; identification with a stepsibling may in fact be easier than with a sibling, because intense sibling rivalry could tend to make it more difficult to imitate someone who has been a competitor for parental love and its symbols. A stepsibling thus can be a more neutral source of identification. The other side of identification is deidentification, and a stepsibling can also prove a more convenient negative model than a sibling. It is more permissible to "hate" a stepsibling than a sibling; because he or she is more emotionally distant it may be relatively easier to take that person as a negative example when establishing one's own identity.

Another positive outcome, stepsibling solidarity, seems to obey the same rules as sibling solidarity. Networks of mutual support apparently develop as children grow into and through adulthood. Issues of competition do not automatically fade with age, but age differences (and with them age-order statuses) do assume less importance as siblings and stepsibling face middle age and old age together. From the case we looked at, and inferring from sibling research, it would seem that stepsibling solidarity in older age is particularly likely between people of the same sex, perhaps because the sexes face these phases of life in different ways.

### Changes in Age Order

When two sets of children are combined into a stepfamily, changes in age order inevitably occur. Age gradations are important for children in their power and status gradations. To alter these positions inevitably requires some children to lose their place in the sibling social order. Thus, the consequences of changing a sibling's place in the age hierarchy really constitute a special case of stepsibling rivalry, but are often dealt with separately, because there has been so much speculation about the importance of age order in intact families, and because it is the only item in stepsibling competition that by definition cannot be equally apportioned. Nothing is known about the long-term effects of alterations of age orders when stepfamilies are formed, but the short-term consequences for children and family are revolutionary, in the sense that an established order of power and privilege is fundamentally altered.

The revolution can take several forms: an only child becomes the oldest, an only child becomes the youngest, an only child becomes a middle child, an oldest child becomes a middle child, and a youngest child becomes a middle child. The evidence discussed suggests possible children's adaptations. Changing from only child to oldest child is probably easiest, because both are privileged statuses. The same may be said for the change from only to youngest. Going from only- to middle-child status is likely to be more difficult because one goes from being on center stage to being lost in the crowd. There are positive and negative aspects to the change from youngest to middle child, to the prince losing his throne. The negative is that it leads to a loss of being the center of attention, whereas the positive is that the child has underlings and people who can look up to him. The most difficult of all the transitions is that of losing the status of being the oldest, because there is such power attached to it; there are compensations, though, in the pressure being reduced. Someone else can be the policeman on the beat.

The negative aspects of changes in age order are resolved by stepchildren's learning to disaggregate their age order in the stepfamily from their biological birth order. A child's adaptation to whatever loss of privilege he or she may have undergone can be enhanced by remembering that no matter what the age order in the stepfamily may be, his place in birth order to his biological parents cannot be altered, and is therefore secure.

### Stepsibling Sex

Sexuality is an even more pressing issue in stepfamilies than in other families, because remarried parents go through their honeymoon in the presence of their children. Even with extremely discreet parental behavior, children cannot fail to be aware of the physical involvement of the adults, although they may not always be certain about what it means. In the worst possible case, children in latency and preadolescent stages will be inappropriately stimulated, which could lead to the arousal of unmanageable and frightening emotions; for adolescents, the stimulation can be even more direct and just as potentially disturbing.

The control of sexuality is thus no less of an imperative in stepfamilies than in other types of families. This is so for stepparent-stepchild sex as well as for stepsibling sex. Yet our culture's mores and the legal system put stepfamilies with stepsiblings in a quandary. On the one hand, sex between stepsiblings is not regarded as incestuous by the law, and is cause for confusion among professionals and parents themselves; there is thus much less of a clear-cut taboo against stepsibling sex than against other types of intrafamily eroticism. On the other hand, as a practical matter a stepfamily cannot permit an active sexual relationship between opposite-sex stepsiblings, because if youngsters are engrossed in such a relationship inside the family, they will not be equipped or inclined to direct their sociability and sexuality outside it. A family that does not train and encourage children to leave it and form their own families and extrafamily adult relationships has, in the profoundest sense, failed as a family. The stepfamily task in this area, then, is to try to manufacture a familial stepsibling incest taboo in the absence of a clear and consistent societal taboo.

Three possible patterns result from this dilemma. One, stepsiblings can engage in sexual activity. The stepfamily cannot properly function for long in this eventuality, and the relationship is likely to be ended by the participants themselves, since most adolescents are not emotionally equipped to deal with such an intimate situation. Much more likely is that erotic feelings will be translated into hostility; hostility is easier to admit, it is less embarrassing, and it is part of the normal attitude of adolescents seeking to separate themselves from their parents. Erotically-inspired stepsibling hostility, however, runs the risk of being more entangling than liberating. Finally, a warm, nonerotic tie can develop between opposite-sex stepsiblings. This sort of outcome is most positive for the everyday functioning of the stepfamily.

Two factors can be tentatively suggested for affecting the probable outcomes. One, of course, is the age of the children when the stepfamily is formed. If opposite-sex stepsiblings are joined together at an early enough age, they will probably develop a de facto stepsibling incest taboo similar to that which develops among unrelated children in the same-age cohorts on Israeli kibbutzim. This leads to the warm, nonerotic tie that is the most positive outcome. To the extent that children are older when the remarriage takes place, the likelihood of another outcome increases. The possibility of stepsibling sexual relations is probably affected by the "sexual culture" of the stepfamily, the overall tone with regard to strict or loose rules for sexual behavior set by the remarried couple. If the sexual culture is permissive, stepsiblings could well take the clue that anything goes. If it is restrictive and discreet, they are likely to avoid sex with each other.

## Half-Siblings

The birth of a child to remarried parents changes the stepfamily from a set of legal ties to a network of blood relationships. It therefore has profound effects on the children as well as the adults involved. We know that the birth of a half-sibling is associated with reports of good adult relations in a stepfamily, although we do not know which causes which. We also know that the presence of a half-sibling has been associated with reportedly good stepsibling relations, although the reason for this, too, is not always clear. One essential component of complex stepfamilies with mutual children is that they have a structural inequality between children. The mutual child has two biological parents in the family, whereas each of his or her half-siblings has only one. One child or set of children is thus inescapably more marginal than another.

Thus there are really two types of half-sibling roles: 1. the half-sibling role of the stepchild; the expectations and behavior patterns of children whose biological parent is parent to a mutual child and 2. the half-sibling role of the mutual child itself. The latter role can be summed up in the concept of being the "hub" of the family, the center around which the family revolves. As a way of approaching the first role, it was suggested that there are stages through which a stepchild must pass in order successfully to adapt to the appearance of a half-sibling: the perception of betrayal and the possibility of renewal.

The birth of a mutual child to remarried parents may be seen as betrayal. This is certainly traceable, at least in part, to the fact that the birth of a half-sibling means that reality is dealing another blow to the children's fantasy of reuniting divorced parents. With a widowed parent, the pregnancy can be seen as a betrayal of the dead. The pregnancy is also a clear testimony to the sexual relations of the parent and stepparent; anger is the result of direct jealousy of the same-sex stepparent as well as the "infidelity" to the ex-spouse that the pregnancy announces. On the other hand, the half-sibling also symbolizes something positive, so after the child is actually born, it is often seen as a sign of renewal. Children often believe that a stepfamily in which there is a network of half-sibling relations is more of a "real" family than the temporary arrangements that remarriage between parents establishes. Finally, the mutual child itself has a position of privilege and power, because the newborn is the center of attention in a stepfamily in a much more intense way than is a newborn in another sort of family. But the privilege is a pressured and precarious one, because the hub bears the weight of the new family on himself. He may feel responsibility for stepfamily events that are beyond his control. Stepfamily cohesion, and sometimes survival, can be seen as the responsibility of a child who has neither commensurate power nor the emotional maturity to withstand serious disruption or a possible breakup of the stepfamily.

What seems to be most important in affecting the quality of stepchild halfsibling relations is age interval. Thus in this case, age probably has a sort of parabolic relationship to difficulties of adjustment, although other factors intervene. When stepchildren are very small, their relationships with half-siblings are likely to be similar to ordinary sibling relations. When the stepchildren are in mid-puberty or older, they are more likely to adopt a quasi-parental role. This role, however, may be tinged with an Oedipal/Electra competition with the stepparent. Quasi-parental competition is more likely if the stepparent is of the same sex and to the extent that the stepchild has spent a long time in a single-parent situation. The likelihood of competition with the stepparent is also greater if the stepchild was an only child in a single-parent situation. Between the extremes of age it is more likely that animosity will develop between stepchildren and the mutual child. These will probably be issues of stepsibling rivalry, another point at which our ideal types overlap.

## Stepsiblings and the Sociology of the Stepfamily

Like stepfamilies in general, stepsibling relations force us to reformulate our thinking about the family. The sociology of the family is only beginning to re-shape itself in response to the changing shape of American families. Here I want to suggest how the issues raised in this book reveal essential outlines for a future sociology of the stepfamily. Such an enterprise will require us to understand how the stepfamily fits into contemporary American society, as well as to analyze the internal workings of the stepfamily.

William Goode has said that the tendency toward worldwide industrialization is being accompanied by a worldwide trend toward the nuclear family.[2] Talcott Parsons goes farther, arguing that capitalism and the nuclear family are mutually adapted. The nuclear family provides early affective support and consequent self-confidence for children, and then later in life encourages an individual autonomy for which the earlier nurturing prepares them.[3] We cannot presume that there is always a perfect match between a given type of society and a type of family, nor that the changes wrought by industrialization are uniform.[4] But since Goode and Parsons made their observations about the congruence of family and society, the U.S. and other societies have entered a newer phase. If the nuclear family is suited to the needs of industrial society, by the same token, the stepfamily may well be suited to those of post-industrial society.

The institution of marriage today has aptly been referred to as "serial monogamy." This state of affairs results from social forces that have long been at work, as sketched at the beginning of the book. Greater longevity, earlier sexual maturity and a wider choice of marriage partners, the proliferation of a service economy, and a declining sexual division of labor have all combined to undermine the life-long, monogamous conjugal family.

These structural social changes have gone hand in hand with changes in mores. Among other things, contemporary American society is characterized by sexual egalitarianism, a stress on instant gratification and consumerism. The old achievement-oriented values that were required for industrializing capitalism have tended to be replaced by a cultural stress on interpersonal competency, other-directedness, and extensive social and sexual experimentation by men and women.[5]

One consequence of these new values is a high divorce rate, and a conception of the family as revolving around what has been called the "eroticized couple."[6] But because our culture still stresses the importance of family life—and perhaps because human beings by nature need stable, continuous intimacy—most divorced parents remarry and form stepfamilies.

However, because these changes are happening so rapidly, there is neither a conventionally accepted public image of the stepfamily, nor is there any scientific theory of the stepfamily, as such. Papernow has provided a framework for understanding the developmental stages through which stepfamilies must evolve in order to be successful; Sager, McGoldrick, and Carter, provide systematic contrasts between nuclear families and stepfamilies.[7] But these sources are therapeutically oriented, aimed at providing useful information to counselors who want to help stepfamilies along. What they do not provide is an actual model of how stepfamilies operate.

In this study, a kind of loose model of the family, based on Parsons' descriptions of the nuclear family as a system within a larger social system, was used as a framework for formulating questions. However, in their internal functioning stepfamilies are so different that borrowing a model in any but the most general sense would be misleading. As Wald says, "the nuclear family, a simple system compared to the remarried family, does not provide an accurate model for understanding interaction in the remarried family."[8]

A functional model of the family was thus used only as a point of departure. The stepfamily was conceived of as a system (quite different in its structure and dynamics from the conventional nuclear family) which has a place in the overall social system, and which has within it several subsystems. This book's focus is on relationships in the *sibling subsystem* within the stepfamily. Stepsibling and half-sibling relations form a unique subsystem within a unique family type—the stepfamily. The stepfamily itself comprises a range of kinship configurations that function, alongside other kinship structures (nuclear families, "single-parent" families, families with cohabiting but unmarried parents) within a post-industrial social structure where kinship itself is relatively marginal, by contrast with preindustrial or industrial society.

The stepfamily thus poses a dual challenge to sociologists—to analyze the functioning of the stepfamily in the larger societal context, and to understand its unique internal processes.[9]

This monograph looked at one aspect of the internal working of the stepfamily. Its conclusions are tentative and hypothetical, and suggest that future research into the stepfamily must undertake two interrelated tasks: 1. to explain the *internal dynamics* of the stepfamily and its subsystems, and 2. to explain the *external functioning* of the stepfamily in the overall social system. The first of these requires a re-thinking of much theorizing about family functioning. Following are some of the suggested directions it must take.

There is no strict functional equivalency between the roles within the nuclear family and those within the stepfamily. This explains the lack of institutionalization of which Cherlin talks, a point particularly underlined by the ambiguous terminology for stepkin.[10] Because they lack legitimacy, obedience to the rules constituting the roles is not routinized. One reason for the lack of legitimacy is the relative novelty of the institution and, until recently, its statistical rarity. Possibly stepfamily functioning will become somewhat smoother when stepfamilies become more numerous. It is also possible that ideological change—from nuclear family to stepfamily ideology—may help this process of stepfamily routinization.[11] This is why some authors and organizations such as the Stepfamily Association of America engage in exercises in legitimation, such as praising stepfamilies and making legislative efforts to have Stepparent's Day made nationally recognized.

However, ideological change can only go so far, and there are irreducible tensions built into stepfamilies that no amount of normative change can assuage. These built-in problems in stepsibling relations were summarized in the foregoing section, but they have broader implications as well.

In nuclear families, the incest taboo means that sex is acceptable outside but not (except for the parents) inside. This is predicated on there being a sharp line of distinction between what is considered to be inside and outside the family. But what used to be done inside the family is now often done outside the family; the industrial revolution moved the place of work outside the family. And in post-industrial society, many family functions are carried on by non-family members—cleaning and other housework, but especially day care and nursery for infants and toddlers. More importantly, the "outside" has been granted admission to the family via remarriage and steprelations.

Another way in which the distinction between family and non-family relations is being blurred by stepfamilies is in the inequalities in wealth between stepsiblings. Because of differences in generosity and financial resources between nonresidential parents and stepgrandparents, there is a kind of class system *within* the family. We are accustomed to seeing whole families located at a certain point in a stratification system, with no internal differentiation of wealth. But the combination stepfamily displays the novel phenomenon of class differences invading the internal workings of the family itself. One type of stepsibling rivalry, therefore, can be thought of as class conflict inside the stepfamily.

The line between intrafamilial and extrafamilial roles is thus increasingly hard to draw. This has potentially profound implications for children's emotional development. Margaret Mead argues that the incest taboo is shrinking because kinship networks are shrinking. The result is fewer areas where intimate, nonsexual development is possible. This, in turn, leads to confusing and unstable marital relationships, to "a kind of corruption of the possibilities of trust and affection, confusing .the children's abilities to distinguish between mates and friends. . ."[12] This is further accentuated by the fact that since children are physiologically entering puberty earlier than ever before, the latency, the "asexual" period during which elementary cognitive and social skills are developed, is getting shorter.[13]

However, these misgivings about the possible pitfalls of internal stepfamily life do not seem to be borne out by evidence regarding the external functioning of the stepfamily. While there may be little internal functional equivalency between stepfamily roles and nuclear family roles, research shows that in American society there is a basic functional equivalency between the stepfamily and nuclear families. Ganong and Coleman, in reviewing the literature to date, conclude that there is little empirical evidence to prove that there are any severe handicaps imposed upon children by stepfamily life in comparison to that in nuclear families.[14] Elsewhere, I have published research showing that there is little difference in long-term adjustment between adults brought up in nuclear families and those brought up in stepfamilies.[15] As far as we now know, stepfamilies are doing almost as well as nuclear families at raising emotionally and socially adjusted citizens.

This leaves us with an apparent paradox. Internally, the stepfamily is a unique institution, unlike conventional families, yet in spite of its oddities, externally it seems to be doing almost as good a job in socializing the young. But the paradox is only apparent. Contemporary American society is characterized by a drastic diminution in the relative importance of kinship. Many social functions previously allocated to family members are carried out by extrafamilial agencies. Thus, while more and more people are being raised in stepfamilies, the relative importance of family life in people's lives is smaller than ever.

The evidence is also mounting that much of personality is shaped by inherited tendencies, both pathological (such as predispositions toward alcoholism) and emotional (such as tendencies toward shyness). Although still important, the patterns of family life are proving to be less crucial in determining personality than was once thought. Whether a child is raised in a stepfamily or a nuclear family may not be more decisive in his ultimate adjustment than his innate personality characteristics.[16]

In short, while stepfamilies may have certain inherent tension in them that nuclear families do not, so many nonfamilial institutions help to socialize children that these strains may not have deep, long-term consequences. And because the stepfamily prepares youngsters for dealing with extrafamilial actors inside the family, as it were, it is preparing them precisely for the intermingling of kin and nonkin that characterizes life in contemporary America. Perhaps stepfamilies do almost as well as nuclear families at raising children in part because the role of the family in raising children, like all kinship in modern society, is so greatly diminished, and because it teaches children that the line between kin and nonkin is not to be considered crucial.

This book is not a manifesto on behalf of stepfamilies, so it has probably offended readers who expected a cheerleading defense of them. It has sought to point out problematic and unresolvable conflicts in stepsibling and half-sibling relations, which are serious but not insurmountable. At the same time, it demonstrates that stepsibling relationships can be sources of joy and personal growth. It has thus probably also offended those who expected a paean to the superiority of the nuclear family. While the evidence discussed suggests that—all other things being equal—it is better to raise children in intact families, when they are raised in stepfamilies they are presented with unique challenges that have their dangers but potential rewards as well.

Certain aspects of stepsibling and half-sibling life are inevitably and normally abrasive. There are foreseeable pitfalls that can either be avoided or successfully negotiated. At the same time, stepsibling and half-sibling relations provide opportunities for new and rich varieties of family experience that are unavailable to children in conventional families. If people can come to see that children in stepfamilies behave in ways that are normal, given the realities that they face, and if people can begin to accept that stepsiblings and half-siblings can nurture one another in new and rewarding ways, then this book will have been a success.

## Notes

1. Max Weber, *Basic Concepts in Sociology*, trans. and ed. H.P. Secher (New York: The Citadel Press, 1964), pp. 52–54.
2. William Goode, *The Family* (Englewood Cliffs, N.J.: Prentice-Hall, 1964), p. 108.
3. Parsons, 1974, "Incest Taboo."
4. Arland Thornton and Thomas Fricke, "Social Change and the Family: Comparative Perspectives from the West, China, and South Asia," *Sociological Forum* 2 (Fall 1987):746–79.
5. Cf. David Riesman, *The Lonely Crowd* (New Haven: Yale University Press, 1950), pp. 116–23, 142–60; and Daniel Bell, *The Cultural Contradictions of Capitalism* (New York: Basic Books, 1975), esp. pp. 65–76.
6. Edward Shorter, *The Making of the Modern Family* (New York: Basic Books, 1977), pp. 245–48.
7. Patricia Papernow, 1984, "Stepfamily Cycle;" Clifford Sager et al., *Treating the Remarried Family* (New York: Brunner and Mazel, 1983); Monica McGoldrick and Elizabeth Carter, *The Family Life-Cycle: A Framework for Family Therapy* (New York: Gardner Press, 1980).
8. Wald, 1981, Remarried Family, p. 88.
9. Ramona Marotz-Baden, et al., "Family Form or Family Process? Reconsidering the Deficit Family Model Approach," *The Family Coordinator* 28, (January 1979):5–14.
10. Cherlin, 1978, *Incomplete Institution*.
11. Cf. B. Fishman and B. Hamel, "From Nuclear to Stepfamily Ideology," *Alternative Lifestyles* 4 (Winter, 1981–82):181–204.

12. Margaret Mead, "Anomalies in American Post-Divorce Relationships," in Paul Bohannon, *Divorce and After,* 1968, p. 107.
13. J.M. Tanner, "Earlier Maturation in Man," *Scientific American* 218 (January 1968):21–27.
14. Lawrence Ganong and Marilyn Coleman, "Effects of Remarriage on Children: A Review of the Empirical Literature," *Family Relations* 33 (July 1984):389–406; also "A Comparison of Clinical and Empirical Literature on Children in Stepfamilies," *Journal of Marriage and the Family* 48 (May 1986):309–18.
15. William Beer, "New Family Ties: How Well Are We Coping?" *Public Opinion* 10 (March/April 1988):14–15, 57; and Kenneth Wilson, et al., "Stepfathers and Stepchildren: An Exploratory Analysis from Two National Surveys," *Journal of Marriage and the Family* 37 (August 1975): 526–36.
16. Jerome Kagan, *The Nature of the Child* (New York: Basic Books, 1984), esp. pp. 240–80; and, for example, Richard Rose et al., "Shared Genes, Shared Experiences, and Similarity of Personality," *Journal of Personality and Social Psychology* 54 (January 1988);161–71.

# Name Index

# Subject Index